LISBETH PERRONE'S FOLK ART IN NEEDLEPOINT AND CROSS-STITCH

Also by Lisbeth Perrone

THE NEW WORLD OF NEEDLEPOINT

LISBETH PERRONE'S NEEDLEPOINT WORKBOOK

THE NEW WORLD OF CREWEL

LISBETH PERRONE'S FOLK ART IN NEEDLEPOINT AND CROSS-STITCH

RANDOM HOUSE   NEW YORK

All rights reserved under International and Pan-American
Copyright Conventions. Published in the United States
by Random House, Inc., New York, and simultaneously
in Canada by Random House of Canada Limited, Toronto.

Library of Congress Cataloging in Publication Data

Perrone, Lisbeth.
Lisbeth Perrone's folk art in needlepoint and cross-stitch.

1. Canvas embroidery—Patterns.   2. Cross-stitch—
Patterns.   3. Folk art.   4. Design, Decorative.
I. Title.   II. Title: Book of folk art embroidery.
TT778.C3P44 1978   746.4'4   78-3710
ISBN 0-394-42401-8

Design diagrams by Nancy B. Roberts
Photography by Neal Slavin
Book design by Kenneth A. Miyamoto

Manufactured in the United States of America

9 8 7 6 5 4 3 2

First Edition

CONTENTS

ACKNOWLEDGMENTS

For making this book possible I would like to extend my thanks and deep appreciation to Yvonne Lange, Director of the Museum of International Folk Art, a unit of the Museum of New Mexico, Santa Fe, New Mexico; to Paul Winkler, Assistant to the Director, and to a very special and long-time friend who has shared her knowledge and encouragement throughout this project, Nora Fisher, Curator of Textiles; and to the entire staff of the museum for their more than cooperative help and good spirits on all occasions, who made me feel welcome and free to pursue my research of the museum's collection at all hours.

I would like to thank my mother, Thomazine Ransjö, and Sylvia Rodgers, Nora Pickens, Charlie Mitchell and Dorothy Shaw for their individual help in embroidering the samplers; and to extend thanks to Nancy Byers Roberts who with skill and craftsmanship provided all the embroidery charts.

The International Folk Art Foundation, the Museum of New Mexico, and the Girard Foundation were generous in allowing me to chart and use some of their folk art embroideries. Grateful thanks are also due to Fredrick Fawcett, Inc., 129 South Street, Boston, Massachusetts, 02111, for providing their linen yarns and the even-weave linen materials that were used for all the cross-stitch samplers.

INTRODUCTION

Not too long ago I passed through Santa Fe, New Mexico, and I was enchanted by the city as well as by the surrounding stark canyons, sun-filled plains, tranquil river beds, adobe walls and forest-covered mountains. The place seemed to strike a special spiritual as well as aesthetic chord for me. Then, when I had the opportunity to look through the embroidered textile collection at the Museum of International Folk Art, I was so taken by the richness and variety of the collection that I was inspired to come back and spend a year studying it and recording it. As I worked, I realized how wonderful it would be if these folk embroideries were adapted so that they could be used by people who embroider today. This book is the consequence of my time in Santa Fe.

The patterns were chosen from a variety of functional articles. There were wedding costumes from Turkey and Palestine, moose-hide shirts from American Indians, ankle bands from China, tablecloths from South America, samplers from Scandinavia and Mexico. . . The Museum is a treasure house of beautiful designs put to functional use by people all over the world.

Folk art is a bond we all share, and now, when we do these designs, we share in the beauty of their creation. Thus, when we choose a pattern for a pillow slip, it may have been used first on a headshawl. You and that craftsman are doing the same stitches and forming the same pattern.

Of course in some instances the colors were changed, or a pattern might have been reduced or enlarged, or had taken from it a particularly attractive element. Basically, though, all the patterns in this book are presented as they were originally executed. All or most of them were done in cross-stitch embroidery. I have charted and chosen patterns that can be done in cross-stitch or in needlepoint on canvas.

All the designs are "figurative." They are of birds, flowers, human figures and animals, and they are adaptable as "repeat patterns." That is, each pattern has a motif that can be repeated as many times as the specific project calls for. The number of repeats will depend upon the size of the finished object and on your own taste. If you wish to make a very clean, open embroidery, you may want to use only one figure on a plain ground. If you want to make a small, overall design, you can reduce the size of the pattern and repeat it many times. You can use the patterns separately or combine them, change or rearrange the color combinations. You can also make any design on any size canvas or on any even-weave material. Just make sure you choose the yarn according to the mesh of your material. For example, if you have a rug in mind, then work on a rug canvas, using a heavy rug yarn. For a piece of clothing or table linen, use a cotton or linen thread on a soft linen.

In addition to the finished articles shown in this book, the patterns can be used for chair seats, belts, wallets, headbands, book covers, picture frames, pincushions, wall hangings, rugs or clothing.

As I became involved with this wonderful collection I tried to define for myself what folk embroidery is. After a lot of thought, I decided that there are many answers and definitions. All embroidery, even the most refined, probably has derived from folk elements, and some folk art embroidery is itself quite refined.

For me, folk art embroidery has several characteristics. It has a purity of design. It is colorful. If the design is for a specific purpose, there is a respect for function and quality. Little-known or anonymous artists are usually involved.

It seems to me that a piece of work becomes folk art when it can express and relate to a heritage, to a historical and social tradition.

And then, of course, there is the joyous spirit of folk embroidery, the tremendous craftsmanship of these artists who had no formal training, the variety of their designs—and the delight there was for me in working with this embroidery. I think you will share that pleasure, especially because these folk art designs also have very practical application. Almost every season, the fashion world introduces some element of folk-embroidered clothing for women, men and children. In recent years there has been a resurgence of folk art embroidery on items for the home—on tablecloths and place mats, on drapery and bedspread borders.

Perhaps as the world around us grows more industrialized and more impersonal, and as we feel less rooted in our own traditions, we have the need to create and re-create this simple, joyous art that belongs to us all.

HOW TO USE AND WORK
WITH THIS BOOK

This workbook contains more than one hundred patterns and motifs. Each pattern can be worked in needlepoint or cross-stitch embroidery. I may have worked one particular pattern in cross-stitch that you would rather work in needlepoint. In that case, just change the background material to canvas, and choose a yarn suitable for the mesh of your canvas. Keep in mind also that when you work on canvas, you will have to pick a color for the background since, in cross-stitch, the fabric usually serves as background. (Of course, if you like a fuller look in your cross-stitch, there is no reason why you can't cross-stitch the background as well.) The same switch-over of materials can be done if rather than my pattern in needlepoint you prefer a cross-stitch project.

To make any of the patterns in the book you need only to be familiar with two stitches, the cross-stitch and the basket-weave, or continental. (The basket-weave and continental are the same stitch, except that the continental stitch is worked horizontally, and the basket-weave is worked diagonally. See stitch directions on page 11.)

Each pattern is shown in full color and has its own work chart done in symbols. Each symbol represents one stitch worked in a particular color. A change of symbol means a change of color.

Some patterns are worked horizontally, some vertically. You can work any pattern or motif in either direction as long as the stitches lie in the same direction. The grid of each work chart represents your canvas or even-weave material. Most charts will show one or more repeats. Note that when a chart extends over more than one page, we have shown an overlap to make sure all the stitches are indicated. Do the stitching on the first page, then pick up the pattern where you left off. The ✻ indicates where to continue stitching.

A few motifs are so big that they can only be shown on the work chart as half a motif. In these few instances, the instructions will tell you to mirror-image the work chart. I tell my students that if they find this technique too complicated, they can simply chart the section of the pattern they have on regular graph paper, using felt-tip coloring pens. The felt-tip pens will absorb clearly through your graph paper. When half the pattern is worked, just turn your graph paper over, and there is your perfect mirror image. I do this whenever I am working with larger motifs. It keeps me from getting "lost" in the counting.

Each pattern is accompanied by a brief history of its folk origin and, where necessary, instructions on how to work the pattern or suggestions for its use.

This book can be used by the beginner, the intermediate and the advanced embroiderer. However, if you are a beginner, start with a modest-sized project. It is a good idea for a beginner to work and complete a few small embroideries. Seeing something finished will lead to grander projects.

What Is Needlepoint?

Needlepoint includes different kinds of embroidery done on a single or double-mesh canvas. For the patterns in this book we have embroidered in quick point and gros point, but any pattern can also be worked in petit point.

Quick point is done on a very coarse canvas, varying in size from 3 to 7 threads to the inch. It is quick to work,

easy to count, and a very good way for a beginner to start "needle-pointing."

Gros point is done on a canvas which has from 7 to 20 threads to the inch. It is the stitch usually called "needle-point."

Petit point is done on a canvas which has more than 20 threads to the inch. It is very delicate work that requires a very fine thread.

What Is Cross-Stitch?

Cross-stitch is also known as **sampler stitch**. It is worked on an even-weave material on which the threads can be counted. The weave of the material varies in size and you should choose it to suit the texture you want. The background of cross-stitch is usually not worked in embroidery, but left open. Keep in mind that when you work in cross-stitch, the design generally will be slightly larger than needle-point as each stitch covers two threads rather than one.

The Stitches*

The Continental Stitch. The continental is a slanted stitch that is always worked from the right side of the canvas to the left. All the stitches go in the same direction (see diagram, far right). When one row is completed,

* Adapted from *The New World of Needlepoint*, Lisbeth Ransjo Perrone (New York: Random House) 1972.

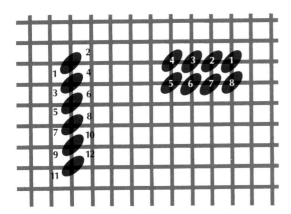

turn the canvas around and come back, working from right to left again. I do not recommend this stitch to cover large areas, since it is likely to pull the canvas out of shape.

There will be times when you will find it necessary to work the continental in a vertical line. In this case, do not work from right to left, but from top to bottom (see diagram, near right).

The Basket-Weave or **Diagonal Stitch.** Basket-weave does not pull the canvas and is appropriate for large background areas. Bear in mind that it can be used with or instead of the continental stitch, since they look exactly the same on the front of the canvas.

This stitch is always worked in diagonal rows, with all the stitches in the same direction. Study the diagram carefully and you will see that the stitches on each row cover every other diagonal crossing of the canvas. Then the returning diagonal row fills in the alternate canvas crossings.

To begin this work, first establish two ordinary continental stitches (1

and 2 on the diagram), one right beneath the other. Now work 3 and 4. You have now established a corner. Next, work 5 and 6 to establish the regular diagonal line of the basket-weave stitch.

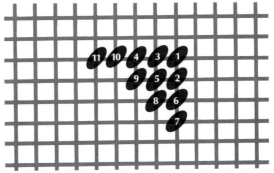

Move from row to row in this manner, adding or subtracting a stitch at the end of the line if you need to change the size of the work. Always work the stitch diagonally back and forth, without turning the canvas. Thus, when you take a new thread, start at exactly the place you left off.

The Cross-Stitch. Cross-stitch should always be worked on a material whose threads can be counted. The crosses should be of even shape and size, and the top stitches should slant in the same direction.

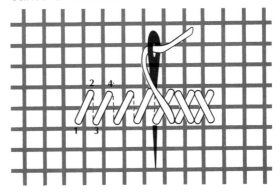

What Tools and Materials Are Needed?

Embroidery basket Keep all your tools and materials in a basket or some other portable storage unit. If not, you will soon find that someone borrowed your scissors or used your yarn to wrap a package.

Needles The needle is the oldest tool of decorative expression, going back to the early Stone Age. Needles used for canvas and cross-stitch embroidery should have a blunt end. They are identified by numbers. Usually the higher the number the finer the needle. An assorted package including sizes from #18 to #22 would be suitable for both needlepoint and cross-stitch embroidery. A darning needle for quick point works very well. Always keep a few extra needles in your storage unit—they do have a way of disappearing.

Scissors Keep two sets in your basket, a heavy pair for cutting the materials and heavier skeins of yarn and a small pointed pair for cutting strands and for "ripstitching."

Thimble Keep a thimble or two with your tools if you are used to working with one. A thimble should be deep and fairly rounded.

Ruler A ruler is good to have for measuring or centering the pattern on your even-weave material or canvas.

Marker Use a permanent marker for indicating lines or marking the center. I find the Nepo needlework marker a reliable one.

Felt-tip coloring pens These are essential if you like to rearrange colors, change a pattern, or easily create a mirror image. (See page 20.) When working with the coloring pens, keep Liquid Paper correction fluid around, as you cannot erase a mistake.

Tape It is always a good idea to tape the edge of your canvas or even-weave material. This will avoid fraying, or the yarn getting caught in the edges. Later, when blocking, you can also place the pins or tacks on the taped edges.

Push-pins These will come in handy when you are ready to block your finished piece. Make sure that they are rust-proof.

Hoop or Frame A hoop or frame is usually not necessary when working on canvas or even-weave materials, but it is like a thimble. If you are used to it, by all means keep a few different sizes in your basket.

Notebook You will be surprised at how many ideas will come to you while embroidering. They will soon be gone if not written down.

Canvas Canvas comes in different widths and degrees of coarseness, and is usually purchased by the yard. The coarseness is graded by numbers. The lower the number the coarser the canvas. Throughout the book we have used canvas #12, except for the quick-point designs, which were done on canvas #5. Of course, as we have said, you can use any size canvas, but do make sure that the appropriate yarn is picked for the size mesh on your canvas. The canvas should be evenly covered. If it shows through the embroidery the yarn is too fine. If the canvas pulls out of shape quite a bit, the yarn is too heavy. However, when working a large piece of needlepoint, one has to expect the canvas to pull out of shape a bit. This is easily adjusted in the blocking process. Canvas is available in a single or double mesh, the latter referred to as "Penelope." I prefer a single mesh, as I find the double mesh to be a strain on the eye. Invest only in the best quality canvas; poor quality will always give poor results.

Even-Weave Materials Even-weaves come in different widths and degrees of coarseness also. Again, the lower the number the coarser the material. For the book we have mainly used #18. The even-weave fabrics are available in different neutrals, as well as lovely pastel colors. This is something to keep in mind, as the background in cross-stitch, done on even-weave, is an integral part of the finished object. I like to work only on even-weaves woven in linens. They are usually imported from Scotland or Scandinavia. As counted-thread embroidery has won more and more popularity over the last few years, you will find that needlework stores throughout the country have started to carry an assortment of even-weave fabrics.

Yarns Not to limit ourselves, we have used a variety of yarns in the samplers. The needlepoint samplers were done in either pearl cotton, regular cotton, 3-ply Persian-type wool, or linen yarn. Sometimes for effect we have embroidered the motifs in one kind of yarn, and then the background in a different type. All the cross-stitch samplers were done in silk or linen yarns. There is something special about linens on linen, but, of course, that does not mean that cross-stitch must be worked with linen threads. Experiment with yarns, but only with those of good quality.

When you pick a thread for your even-weaves, a good rule to remember is to pick one that is equally coarse or fine as the warp and weft thread in the material. You will then have a nice fullness to your stitches. Needlepoint will require quite a bit more yarn than a cross-stitch embroidery. When I estimate the amount of yarn needed for a needlepoint project, I figure roughly one yard of thread for each square inch and then I allow for some extra yarn. It is better to have some left than to end up not being able to match a color. Also, do make sure that you get the same dye lots if a project calls for a larger quantity of a particular color.

How to Start a Project and Read a Chart

When you have decided what kind of project you want to do, browse through the book and pick a pattern that you like. Keep in mind where the finished article is going to be placed, hung, sat on, or put to use.

It is now time to obtain your background material and yarns. Remember, poor quality will give poor results. Consult your local needlework store as to the amount of yarn for a given size. Test the yarn with your canvas or even-weave material before you buy larger amounts of it. Make sure that you get enough yarn, and allow at least an extra 2 inches of canvas or fabric all around for blocking and mounting.

Next, put masking tape around the edges. With your permanent pen, mark the center as well as the outline of what is going to be the actual size of the finished piece. You can find the center by using a ruler or by lightly folding the material in half first horizontally, then vertically. Where the two folds intersect, put a mark with your permanent pen. You now have the center.

Always start the center of a repeat in the center of your background material. This way, the repeats will be evenly arranged on the finished piece.

Now, look at the chart. Each symbol represents one stitch done in a par-ticular color. There is a color key next to the chart showing how many colors were used for that particular pattern. Allow each color its own needle. It is easier to work with a few needles because rethreading the needle each time is tedious and time-consuming.

When you have color-keyed a pattern that calls, for example, for blue, red and green, put together tones of these colors that please you. The color photographs will, of course, guide you in the selection of yarns, but there are such nuances of color available that you should choose those which seem to you to harmonize best.

If there are any instructions with the chart, take the time to read them either for help or for some better understanding of the pattern.

When you are ready to start embroidering, keep these few hints in mind: never knot your yarn; fasten it by weaving it in and out on the back of your work. If you work in cross-stitch, fasten your thread in the direction of the stitches; the fastened thread may otherwise show through on the front. The thread that you are working with should not be more than 18 inches long. A thread can be carried on the back from one place to another, but no farther than one inch. Don't pull the yarn too tightly, but try to establish an even rhythm with the stitches. If the yarn gets twisted while you're working, hold your material up in the air and let the threaded needle hang down. It will unwind itself the way a telephone cord does.

Follow the chart carefully. If you decide to change the colors, I suggest that you rechart the pattern, using the felt-tip coloring pens. It will be easier to follow and less confusing. A graph paper that has ten squares to the inch is a good size to chart on. As you work your pattern, keep checking back with the chart. A mistake is so easily made, and no one enjoys "ripstitching" very much.

How to Finish Your Embroidered Piece

When you have finished the actual embroidery, three steps are necessary to complete your project—checking, blocking and mounting.

First, check your work carefully. By holding it up to the light you will soon discover if there are any missing stitches. If you find any, fill them in. Make sure that all the threads are carefully fastened and secured on the back. Trim the back by clipping unnecessarily long threads, but don't clip so closely that the embroidery unravels.

Check the front carefully too for a stitch that has looped or worked loose on the front. If so, pull the stitch to the back and secure it with another thread. When your embroidery has been carefully checked, take some strands of each color you have been working with and set it aside for re-

pair purposes. If the finished embroidery is going to be mounted, I always attach these extra strands, loosely, to the back of my work. This way, they will always be there, and might come in handy at some future date.

Most embroidered pieces will then have to be blocked. If you do a fair amount of embroidery, take the time out to make a blocking board. I use a piece of insulating wall board which has enough give to push tacks or pins into. Glue or staple graph paper to the board and then wrap the board with a piece of plastic to keep the paper from getting wet. When blocking, start by dipping a clean sponge into a mild soap solution, like Ivory soap, and go over the entire back of your work until it is thoroughly dampened. Do not press or rub. Treat your embroidery gently. Now lay the embroidery face up on the blocking board. Using the graph paper as a guide, tack the dampened embroidery down at quarter-inch intervals with rustproof pins or tacks. When the embroidery is thoroughly dry, remove it from the board. If it is still a bit out of shape, repeat the same procedure.

When working with a piece done in cross-stitch, you might not have to do any blocking at all since this stitch doesn't tend to pull the material out of shape. Light pressing with a dampened pressing cloth is usually sufficient.

After you have used the embroidery for a while and it soils, you can use the "Ivory method" to clean your embroideries. As your pieces are likely to be framed or mounted, you will have to clean them gently from the front. Another method which I successfully used for years is to cover my embroideries with a fiberglass screen. Then, using a vacuum cleaner, gently go over the mesh covering the embroidery. The dust and dirt will be picked up without damage to the stitches.

If you want to mount your own work, consult one of the very good books on this subject. Your work can also be mounted professionally. Consult your local needlework store or department store. They will usually do it for you; if not, they can refer you to someone who can.

Another way to approach the problem is that in needlework stores throughout the country you will find ready-made articles with blank canvas inserted. Whenever I can, I use these already finished articles. Most of them are well made, and they will often save both time and money.

Applying a Pattern to Other Fabrics

I often hear from a student that she or he would like to embroider a cross-stitch design onto a blouse, jacket,

pair of pants, or make a border on plain linens like a sheet or pillowcase. But how? Does the material have to have a stamped design or be an even-weave material? No, not at all. Just baste a piece of Penelope canvas, *noninterlocking*, onto what is going to be enriched by embroidery. Work the cross-stitches over the canvas and through the fabric. When the embroidery is finished, dampen the interlocking canvas and embroidered part, and with a pair of tweezers pull away the interlocking threads, and you are left with the embroidery only. Needlepoint stitches can be used as well, although in my opinion a cross-stitch will look fuller and does adapt better. Any of the patterns in the book can be applied and used this way, without canvas or even-weave.

Creating Your Own Color Combinations

Perhaps a particular pattern in the book has caught your eye, but the colors we've used are not suitable for what you have in mind.

Don't worry. You'll find, once you begin, that it is fun and easy to arrange your own combinations. The palette you have to work from includes the primary colors: red, blue and yellow; as well as secondary colors: purple, green and orange. There are, however, many, many tones between

pages 20-21

page 19

page 19

page 22

page 22

1

page 23

page 24

page 27

page 28

page 27

page 25

page 26

page 29

III

pages 30-35

page 37

page 36

page 38

page 36

page 39

page 39

IV

pages 40-47

pages 48-49

pages 48-49

V

page 54   page 53   page 53

page 51

page 50

page 51

page 50

page 52

page 52

VI

page 55

page 56

VII

pages 57-59

page 61

page 60

page 60

page 61

VIII

these colors that are almost impossible to exactly describe.

There are no rules for putting colors together but I have found that nature is a wonderful source of inspiration. Even when nature juxtaposes the most unorthodox combinations, they look beautiful. I keep a good supply of garden catalogs around, and many of my own combinations of color are a direct steal from one of these.

Try to be free and adventurous with color in your embroidery. The finished piece should be able to live in the environment where it is going to be used or seen, but the most important thing is that its colors look right to you.

THE DESIGNS

From a dress, Ramallah, Palestine

Background magenta (dark pink)
Design steel grey ◆
  yellow ○

From front of an embroidered dress, this would adapt nicely to upholstery.

Color illustration page I.

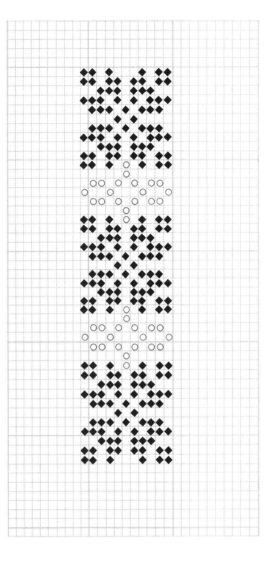

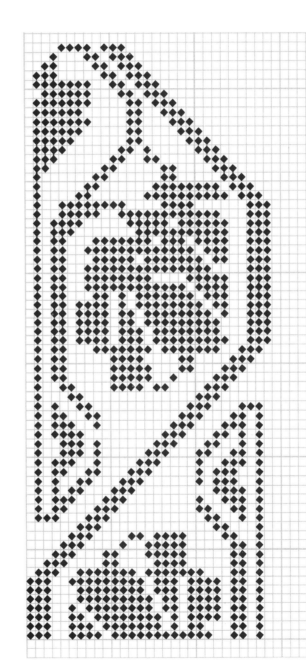

From a bride's dress, Palestine

Background light purple
Design dark green ◆

One of my favorites, this Palestinian piece resembles an Art Nouveau design.

Color illustration page I.

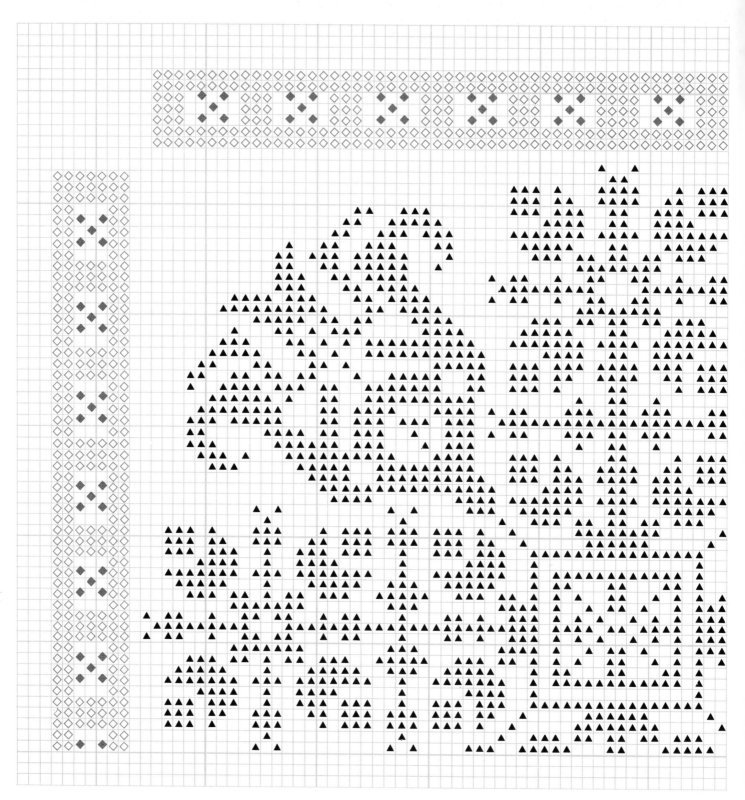

From a pillowcase, Hungary

Background even-weave linen fabric
Design red ▲
blue ◇
green ◆

20

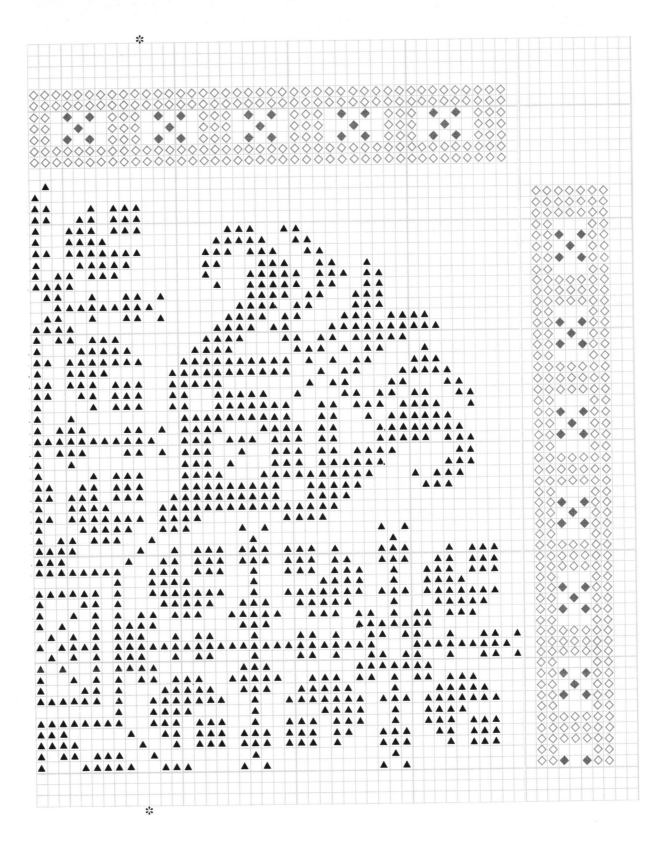

This cross-stitch pattern is reminiscent of many
European designs and is worked in mirror images.
See page 9 for instructions on overlapping
charts.

Color illustration page I.

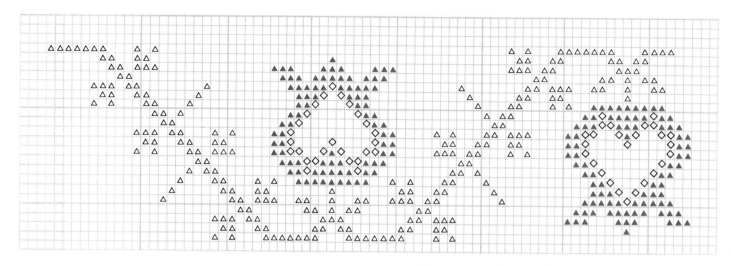

From a sampler, Puebla,* Mexico

Background   maroon
Design   light blue   ◇
         dark green   △
         red   ▲

This looks like a Mexican valentine. Use either vertically or horizontally.

Color illustration page I.

* *A state in Central Mexico, also the name of the capital of this state.*

From an ankleband, China

Background   maroon
Design   black   ◇
         pink   ●
         turquoise   ▲

Chinese inventiveness put this on a lady's ankle, but it is a wonderfully practical design.

Color illustration page I.

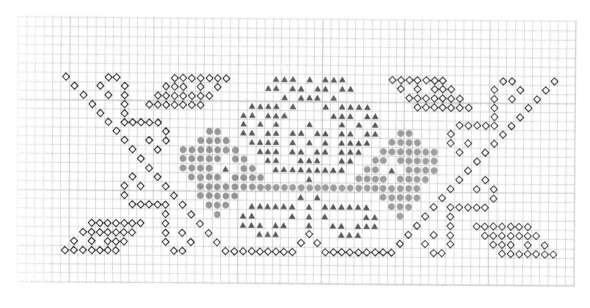

From a boy's costume, Huichol tribe, Mexico

Background   yellow   ◇
Design   red   △
         blue   ◆
         green   ●

We have worked this design on a pre-made skirt, available in most art-needlework stores.

Color illustration page II.

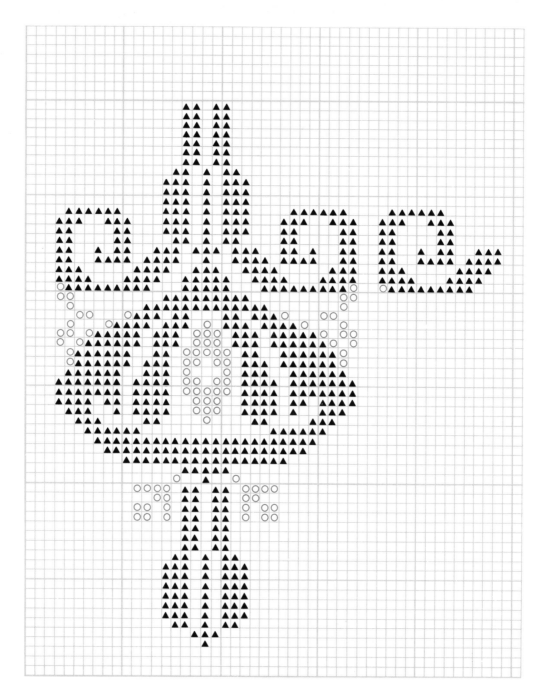

From a runner, Czechoslovakia

Background   black
Design   light pink   ○
         magenta   ▲

A bold pattern, effective as a border
on a curtain or a bedspread.

Color illustration page III.

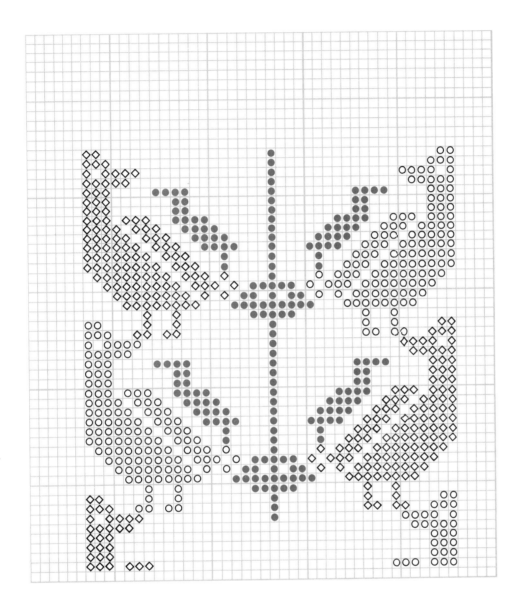

From a woman's dress, Palestine

Background   black
Design   light green   ●
          turquoise   ◇
          deep pink   ○

These mama birds and babies would make
a charming needlepoint rug or hanging.

Color illustration page III.

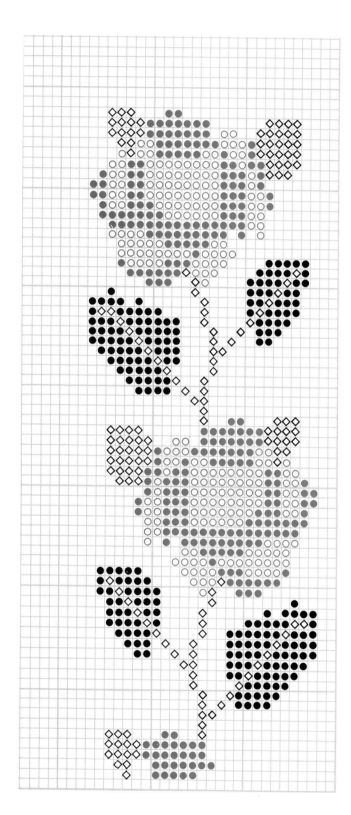

From a sampler, New Mexico

Background   blue
Design   pink   ○
         red   ●
         olive   ◇
         light green   ●

A late nineteenth-century pattern. We have reversed the roses.

Color illustration page III.

26

From a woman's dress, Palestine

Background   purple
Design   orange   △
         white   ●

We have used this as a border on a dress, but it would also be lovely in any all-over pattern.

Color illustration page III.

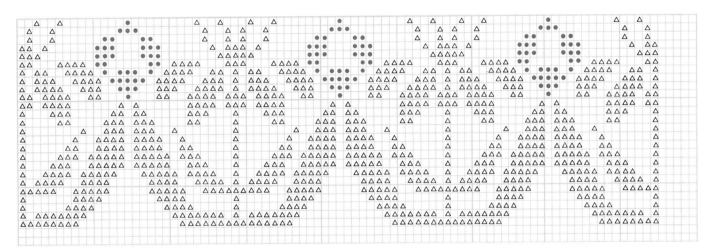

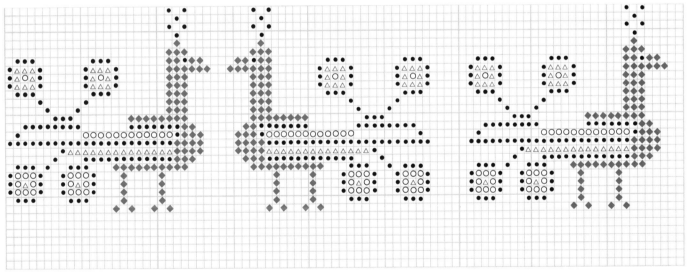

From a sampler, Holland

Background   blue
Design   pink   ◆
         light blue   ●
         rust   △
         yellow   ○

Do you think these are Dutch peacocks?

Color illustration page III.

From a sampler, Puebla, Mexico

Background   orange
Design   green   ◇
white   ●
purple   △
blue   ▲
yellow   ◆

A soft flower worked with a bold background.

Color illustration page III.

**From a man's costume, Huichol
tribe, Mexico**

Background   blue
Design   bright yellow   ●
            cream   △

A butterfly that can be used alone or in a flock.

Color illustration page III.

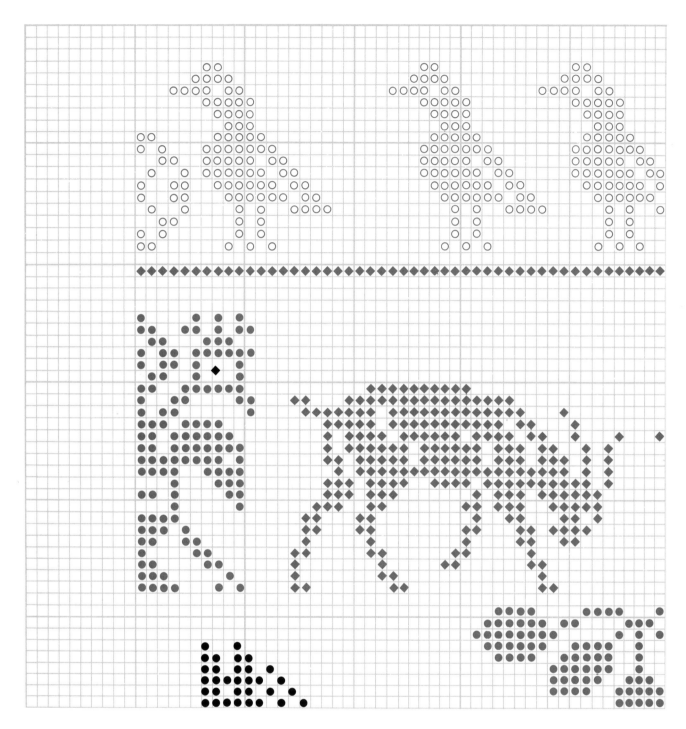

**From 2 samplers, Mexico and a
Bag, Mexico**

Background   even-weave linen fabric
Design   dark green   ▲
         yellow   ◆
         rust   ●
         grey   ○
         beige   ◇
         orange and
         maroon   ○
         dark purple   △
         blue   ●

The diagram for this design
continues through page 35.
See page 9 for instructions
on overlapping charts.

30

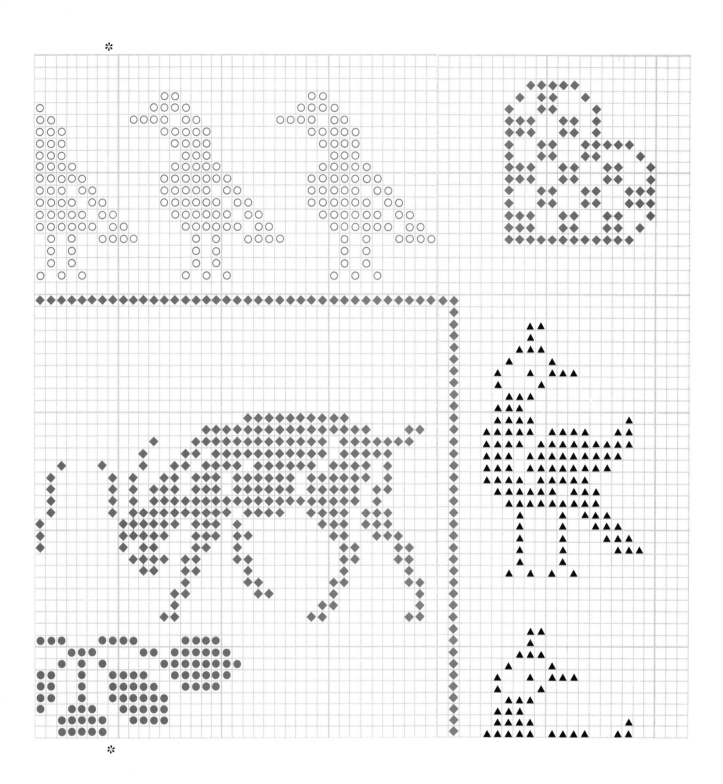

Here we used several Mexican pieces and our
own adaptations to tie all the animals together.
Of course you can use any one of these animals
in an overall design for something like
a chair seat or pillow.

Color illustration page IV.

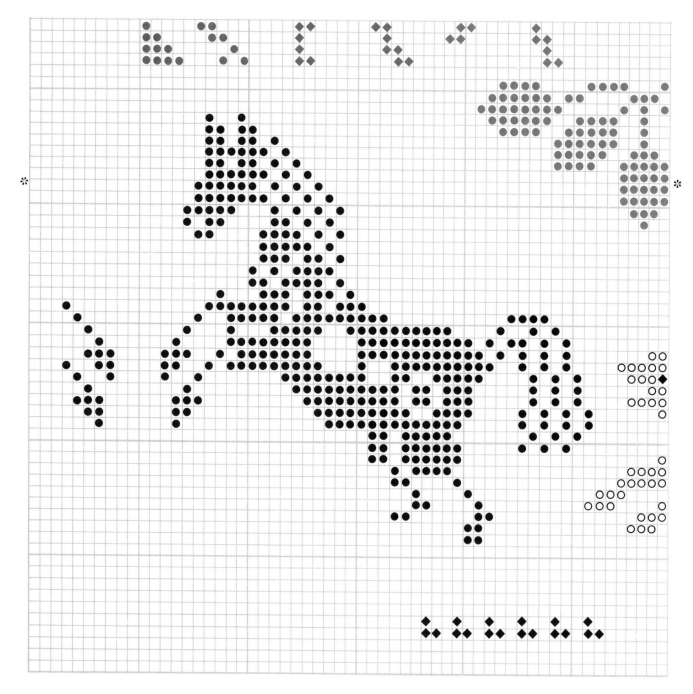

Design   dark green   ▲
           yellow   ◆
           rust   ●
           grey   ○
           beige   ◆
           orange and maroon   ○
           dark purple   △
           blue   ●

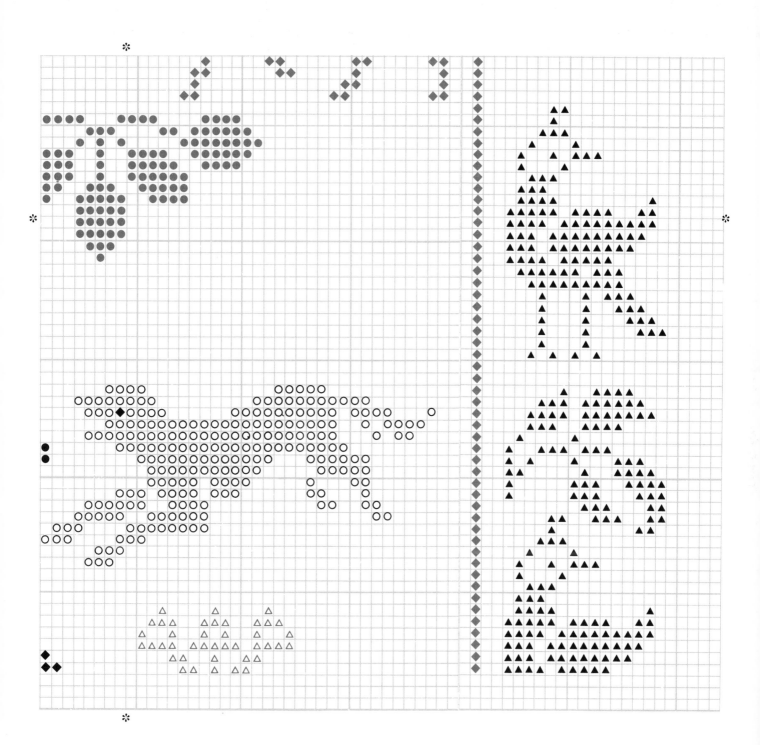

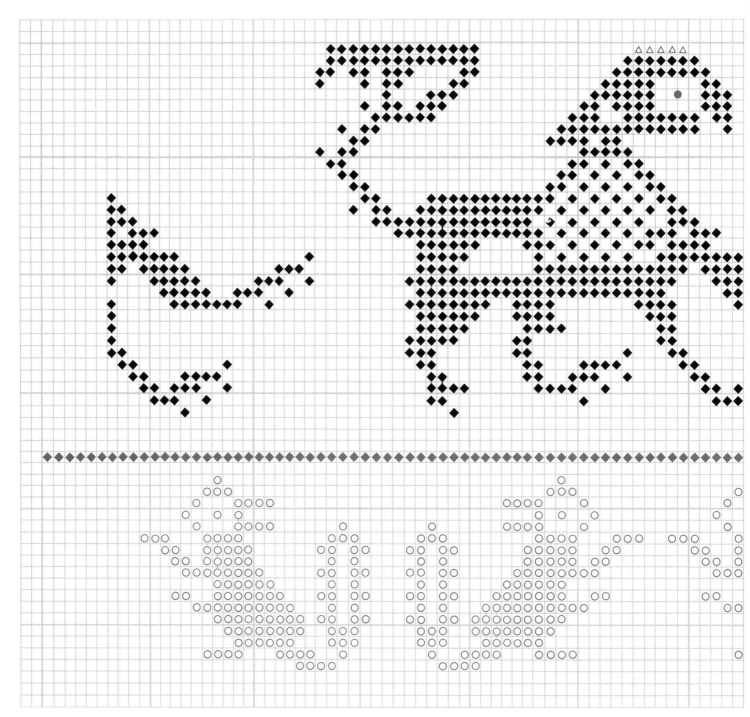

Design   dark green   ▲
          yellow   ◆
          rust   ●
          grey   ○
          beige   ◆
          orange and maroon   ○
          dark purple   △
          blue   ●

34

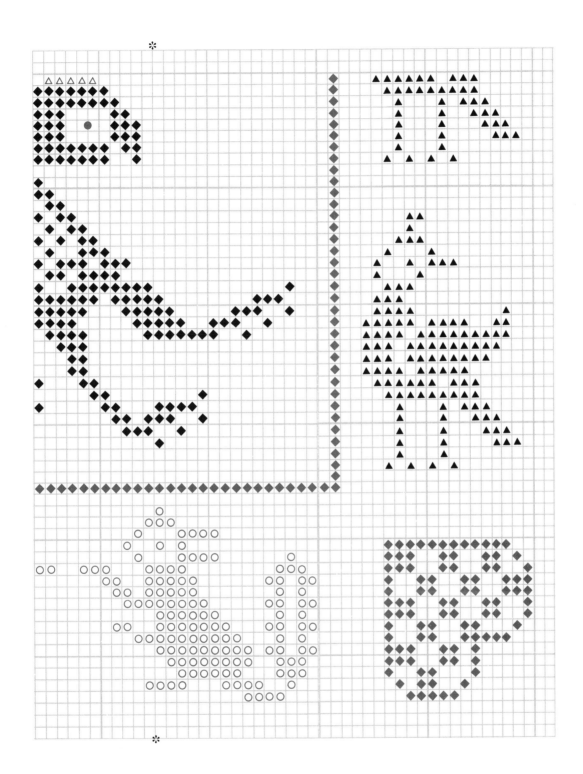

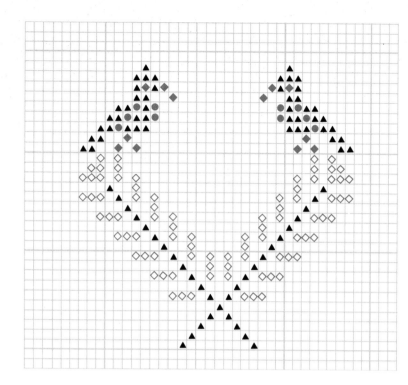

From a sampler, Mexico

Background white
Design dark green ▲
       blue ◆
       light green ◇
       red ●

Again, to accentuate a very small design we have used a heavy canvas and yarn, but you can work more delicately.

Color illustration page IV.

From a sampler, Holland

Background white
Design light green ○
       scarlet red ◆
       purple ▲

You might use this as a wedding embroidery with the bride's initials on the left, the groom's initials on the right.

Color illustration page IV.

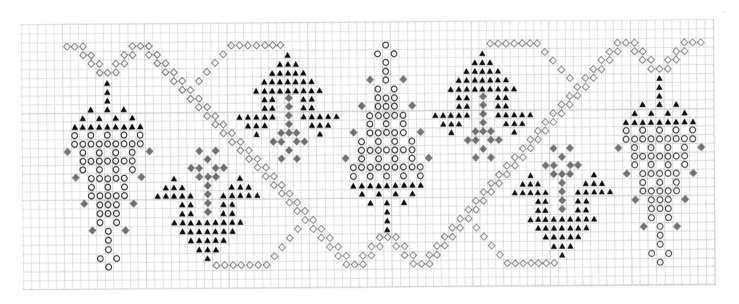

From a sampler, Puebla, Mexico

Background   ecru
Design   green   ◇
         brown   ▲
         red   ◆
         orange   ○

An autumn-like design I have used as
a border on a slipcover.

Color illustration page IV.

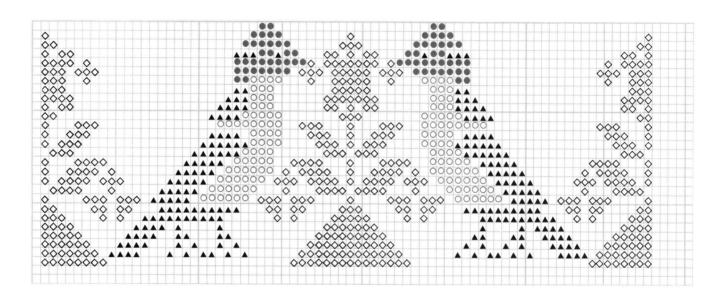

From a sampler, Mexico

Background   yellow
Design   purple   ◇
          black   ▲
          dark blue   ●
          light blue ○

Charming birds like these appear on folk art
samplers throughout the world.

Color illustration page IV.

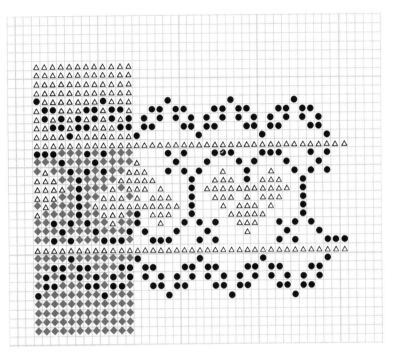

From a sampler, Guatemala

Background   none
Design   red   △
         dark green   ●
         yellow   ◆

A Christmasy design with a Latin American touch.

Color illustration page IV.

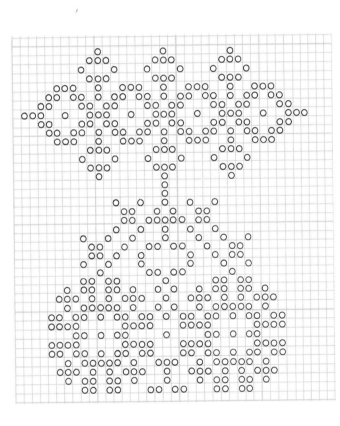

From a sampler, Hungary

Background   lemon-yellow
Design   purple   ○

Hungary is famous for the use of bold colors in embroidery. Here we have used more subtle colors and you can, of course, experiment to suit your own mood.

Color illustration page IV.

From a sampler, Mexican–1862

Background   even-weave linen fabric
Design   dark green   ◆
          light green   ○
          purple, magenta   ●
          gold   △
          dark blue   ●
          light blue   ○
          brown   ◇
          beige   △
          orange   ▲

40

We think this nineteenth-century sampler is one of the loveliest. We expanded it by repeating or reversing some of the figures. Use it as it is shown, or pick up individual elements to create your own pattern. (Please note that the chart simplifies the colors in the photograph a bit.)

Color illustration page V.

The diagram for this design continues through page 47. See page 9 for instructions on overlapping charts.

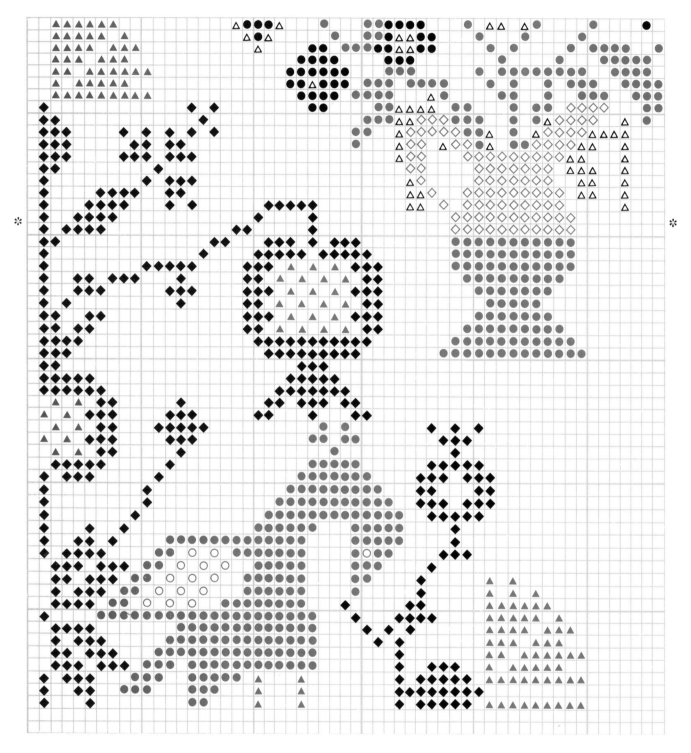

Design dark green ◆
        light green ○
        purple, magenta ●
        gold △
        dark blue ●
        light blue ○
        brown ◇
        beige △
        orange ▲

42

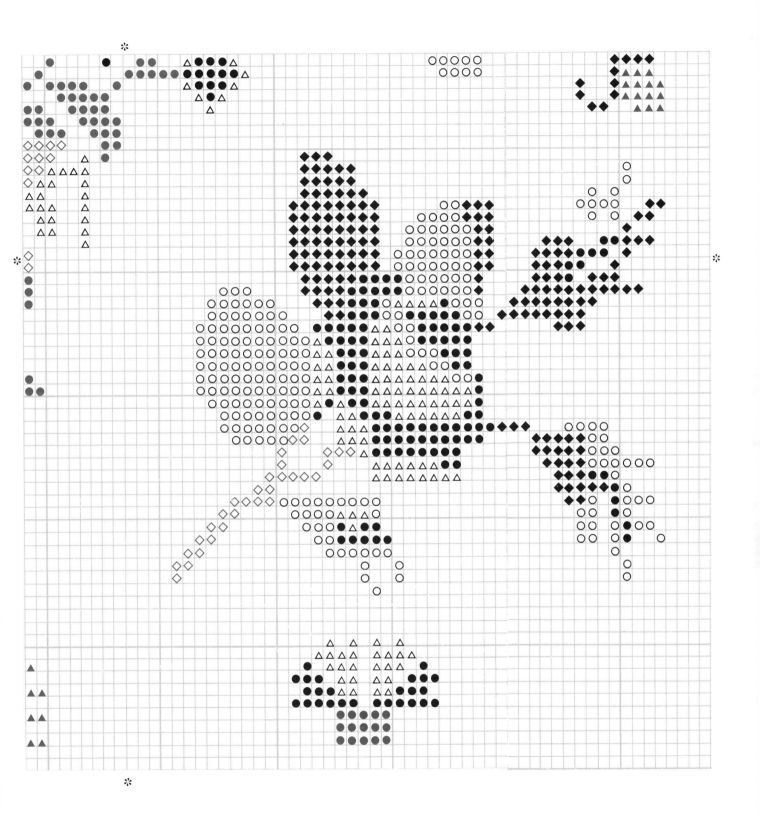

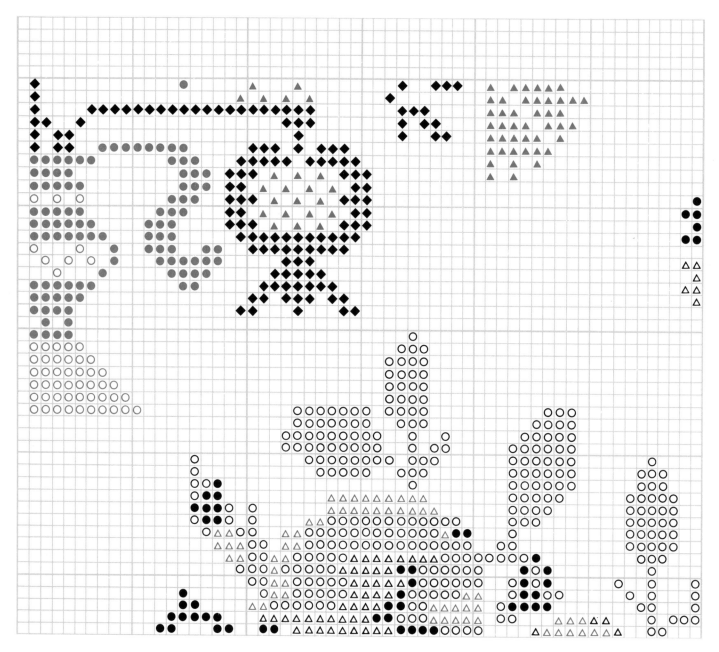

Design   dark green   ◆
          light green   ○
          purple, magenta   ●
          gold   △
          dark blue   ●
          light blue   ○
          brown   ◇
          beige   △
          orange   ▲

44

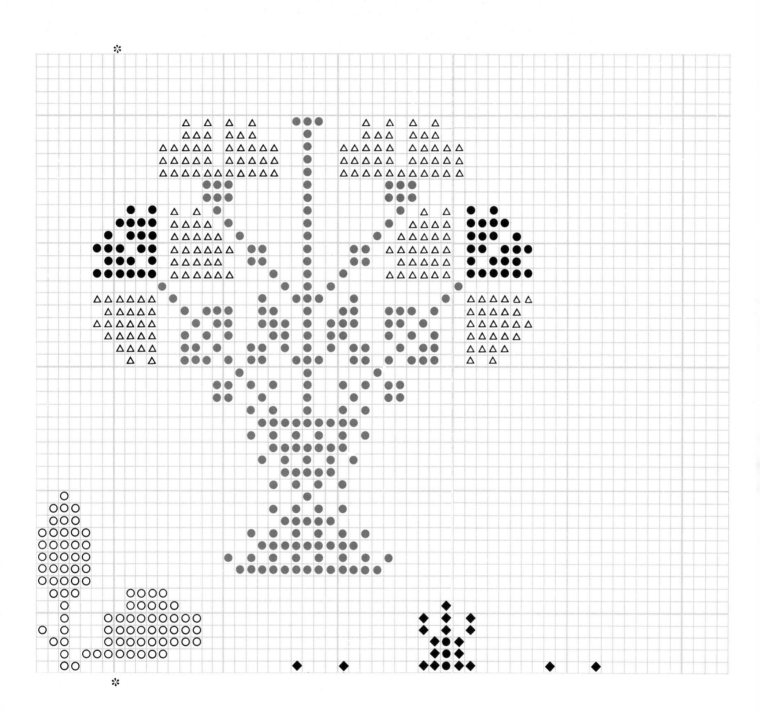

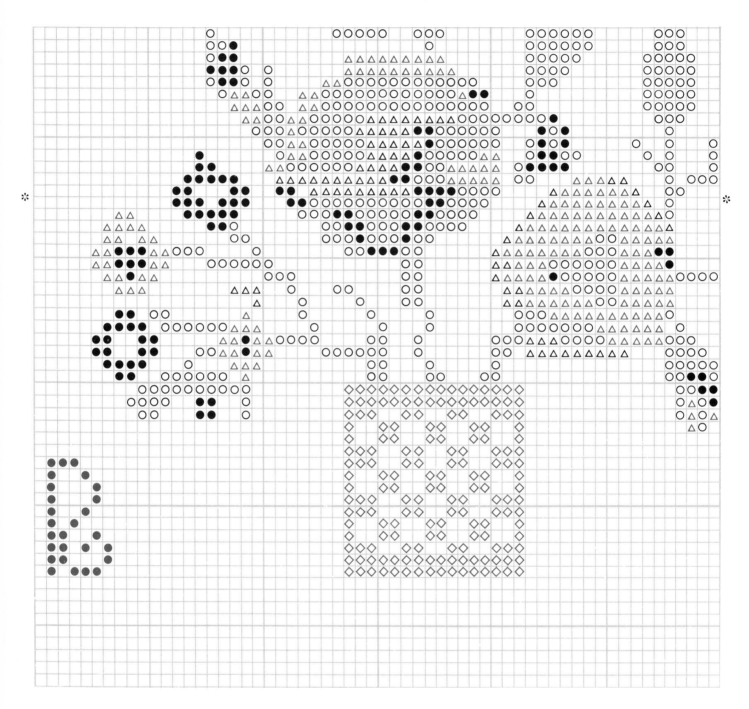

Design   dark green   ◆
          light green   ○
          purple, magenta ●
          gold   △
          dark blue   ●
          light blue   ○
          brown   ◇
          beige   △
          orange   ▲

46

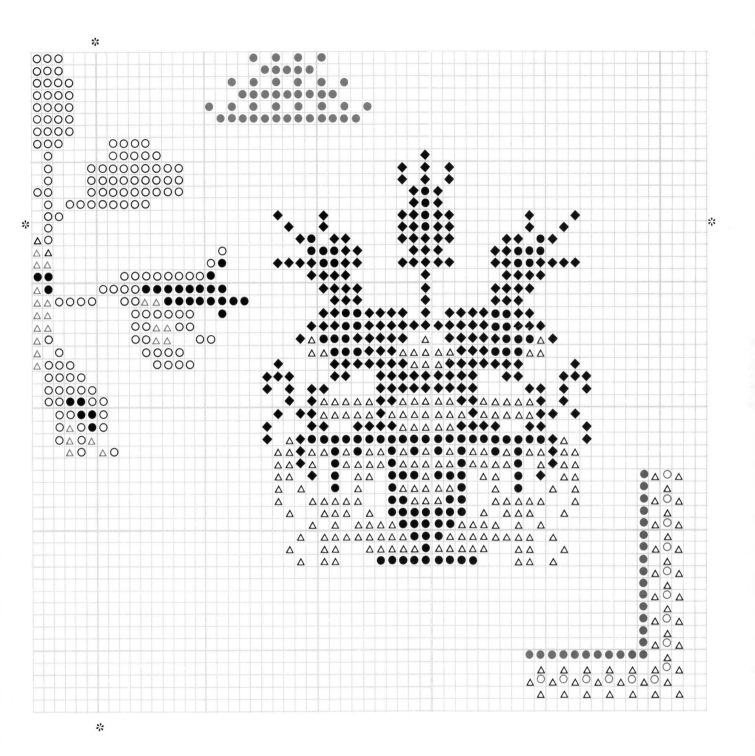

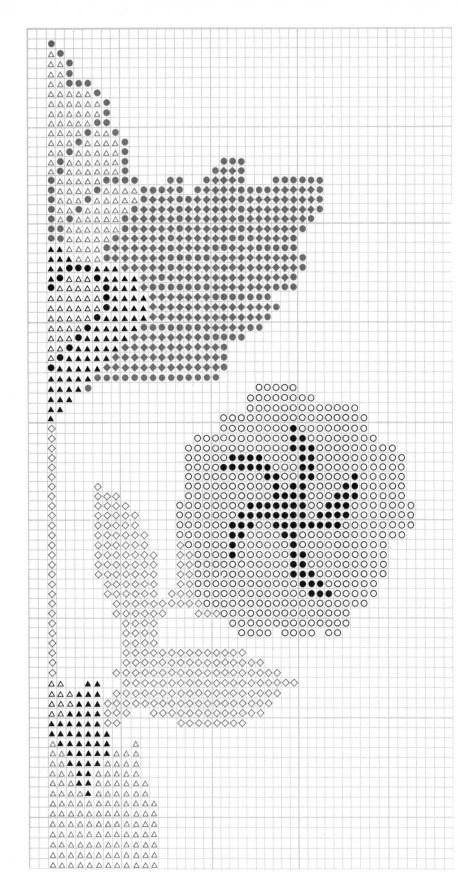

From a jacket, beaded, moosehide, Cree, Chippewa*

Background
  for needlepoint   light blue
  for cross-stitch   even-weave
                      light-blue linen
                      fabric

Design   blue   ●
          red   △
          magenta   ▲
          orange   ○
          light pink ◆
          dark green △
          olive green ◇
          black   ●
          light green ◆
          white   ○
          yellow   ▲

We have done this design in needlepoint on canvas and cross-stitch on even-weave linen just to show you again how the designs adapt to both techniques. In fact, it was originally done in beads on moosehide. Wouldn't it be wonderful to try to embroider in beads? You could use these same charts to do it. See page 9 for instructions on overlapping charts.

Color illustration page V.

* A member of an American Indian people of Ontario, Manitoba, Saskatchewan and Montana. Chippewa itself stands for an Athapaskan language of Northwest Canada.

pages 62-70

page 71

page 72

page 73

page 72

page 77

page 76

page 75

page 74

page 76

page 75

X

page 78

XI

page 80

page 79

page 79

XII

page 82

page 81

page 82

page 80

page 81

page 83

XIII

pages 85-89

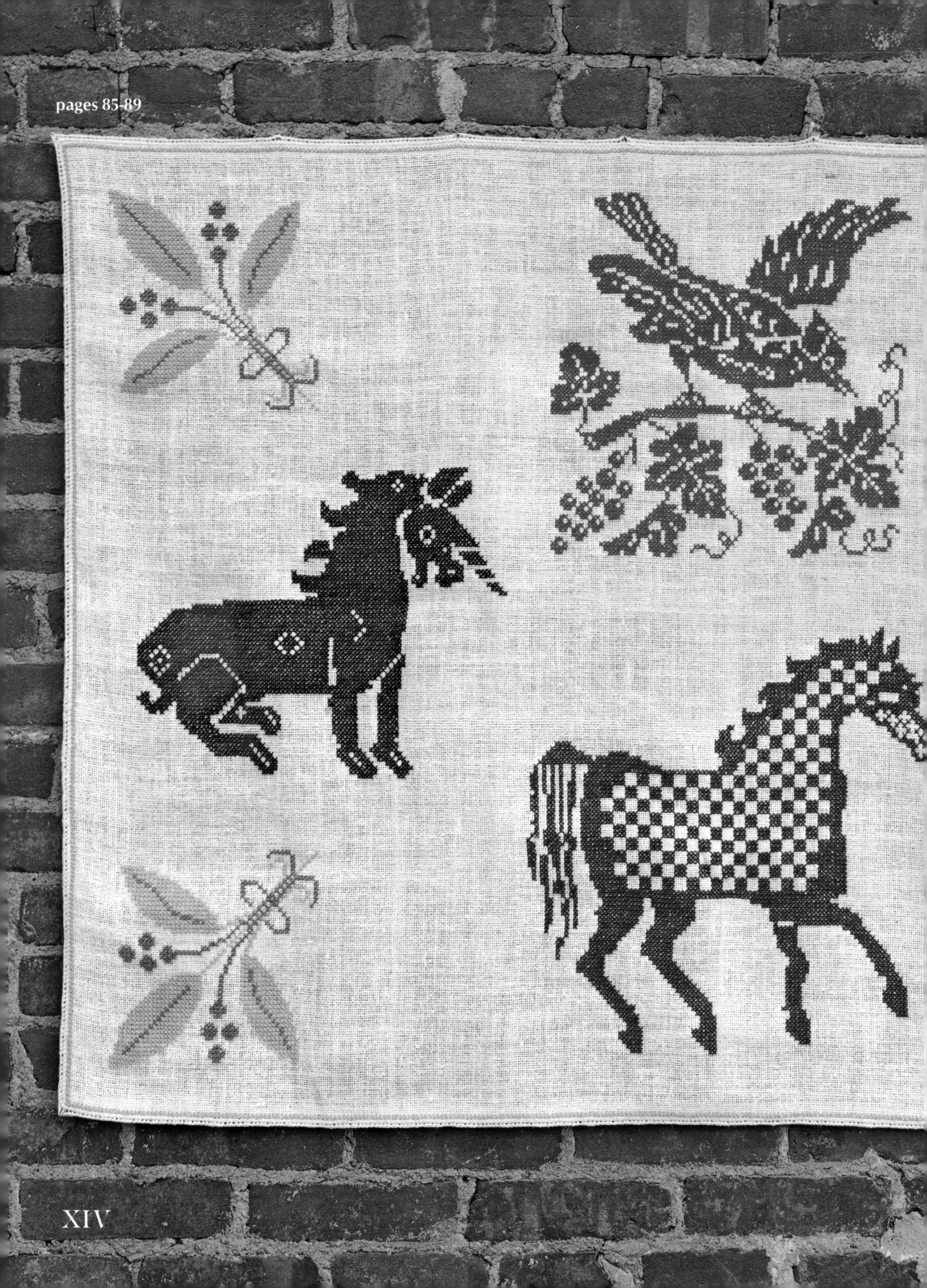

page 89

page 84

page 84

page 85

page 83

XV

page 90

page 91

page 92

page 93

page 94

page 95

page 90

XVI

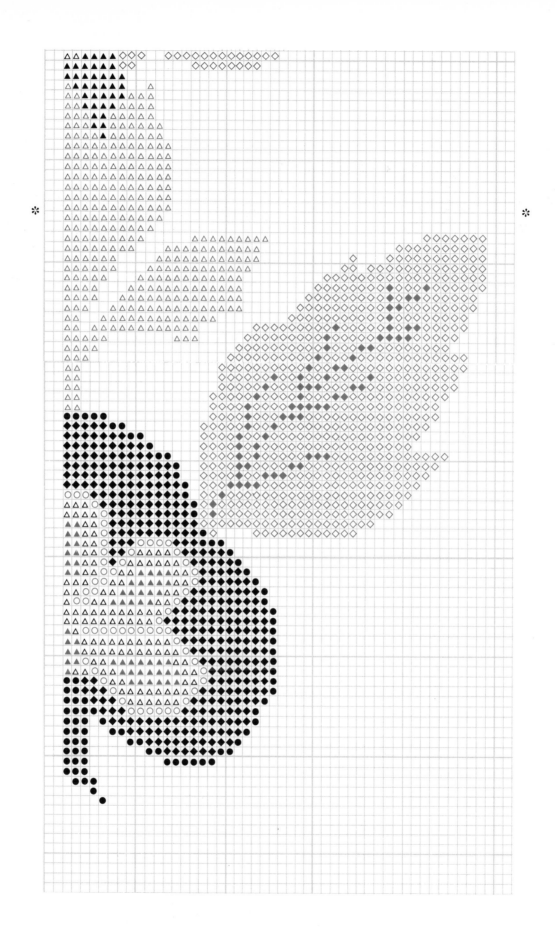

From a sampler, Mexico

Background   yellow
Design   dark brown   ◆
           light brown   △
           ecru   ○
           orange   ●

These have a ceramic look to them and would
make an interesting design repeated in mirror
image.
Color illustration page VI.

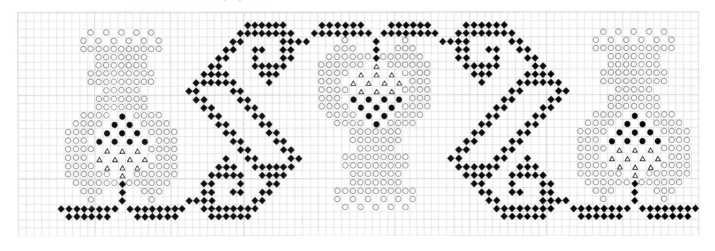

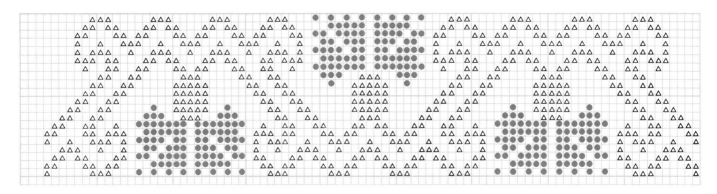

From a sampler, Guatemala

Background   dark brown
Design   grey   △
           pink   ●

Unusual colors give this folk design real elegance.

Color illustration page VI.

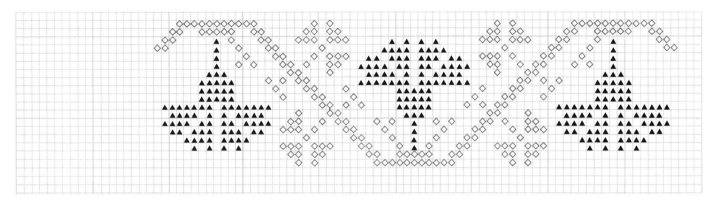

From a sampler, Mexico

Background   dark brown
Design   peach   ▲
          green   ◇

Carnations for a delicate piece.

Color illustration page VI.

From a sampler, Mexico

Background   dark green
Design   red   ●
          light green   ◆
          yellow   △
          light blue   ○

Leaves and flowers are linked together here.

Color illustration page VI.

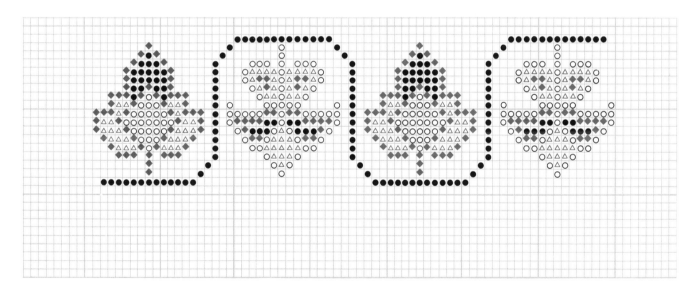

**From a sampler, New Mexico
late nineteenth century**

Background   gold
Design   rust   ○
          aqua   ◆

On a white background, instead of yellow, you
would get a nice Christmasy effect.

Color illustration page VI.

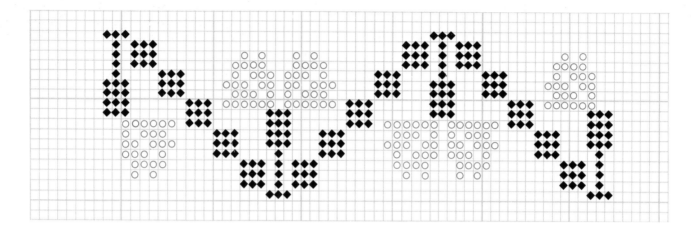

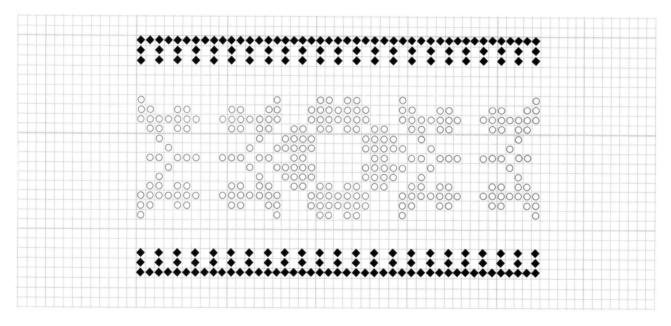

From a bride's dress, Palestine

Background   green
Design   magenta   ◆
          light pink   ○

You could embroider these in cross-stitch over
gauze to delicately decorate a girl's blouse.

Color illustration page VI.

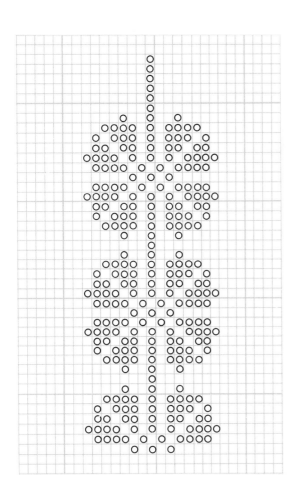

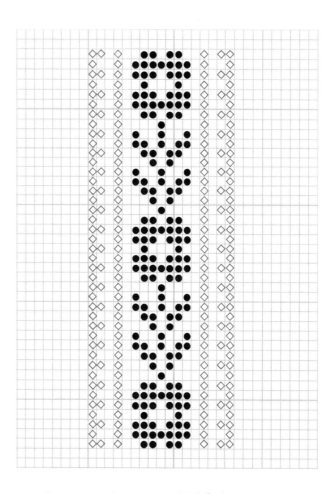

From a headshawl, Palestine

Background brown
Design yellow ○

This is like a lollipop of pattern and is both decorative and amusing.

Color illustration page VI.

From a man's costume, Huichol tribe, Mexico

Background orange
Design dark blue ◇
light blue ●

Eliminate the "frame" of stitches if you want to use these flowers in an overall design.

Color illustration page VI.

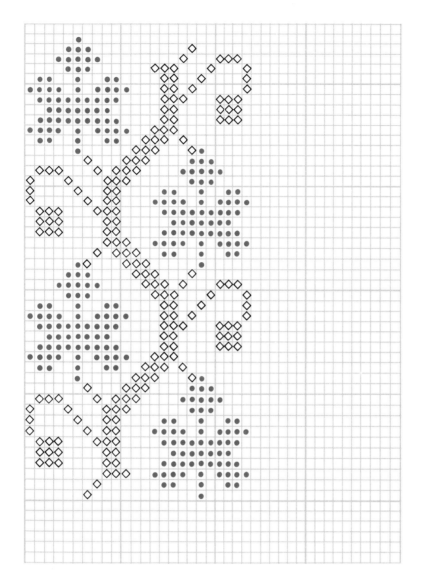

From a sampler, Mexico

Background   turquoise
Design   dark brown   ◇
            orange   ●

The turquoise background is unconventional but accents the pattern beautifully.

Color illustration page VI.

**From a tablecloth, Mexico
(Gerard Foundation)**

Background   bright green
Design   red   ▲
            black   ○

A covey of mythological birds that would also be charming for a child's picture.

Color illustration page VII.

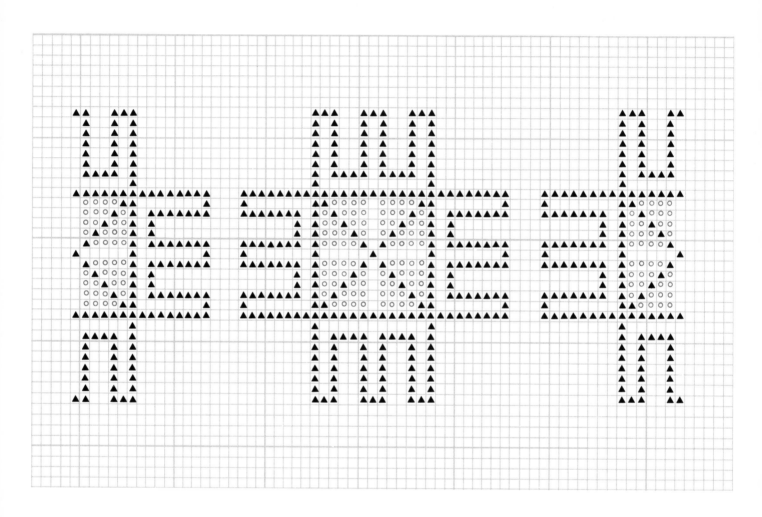

From a dress, Ramallah, Palestine

Background   bright green
Design   blue   ▲
          red   ○

Most people think this Palestinian design is from
New Mexico. Isn't it amazing how universal folk
patterns are?

Color illustration page VII.

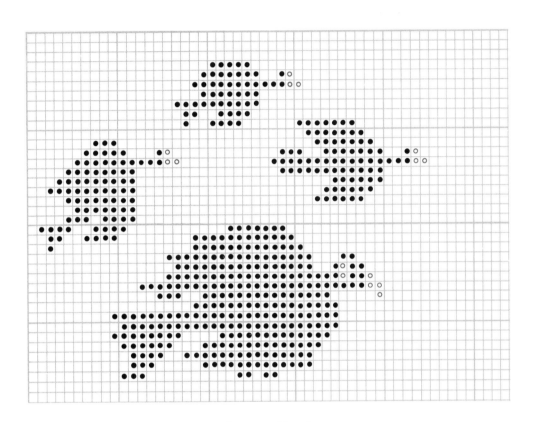

From a sampler, Scandinavian

Background   a closely woven linen fabric
Group of birds   gray   ●
                  dark brown   ○

We have used cross-stitch over gauze (see color
page X) on all clothing. Most of the clothing in
the book was bought ready-made. The only
exception is the dress on color page XI.

Color illustration page VIII.

Sections of this design continue to page 59.

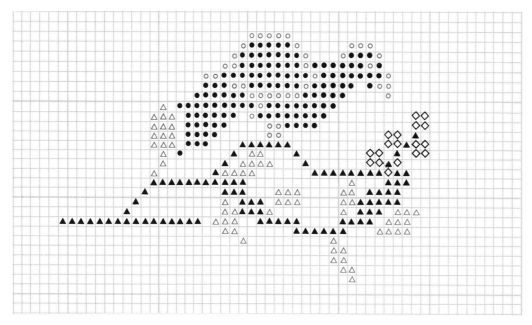

Single bird   gray   ●
                dark brown   ○
                blue-green   △
                light blue   ▲
                pink   ◇

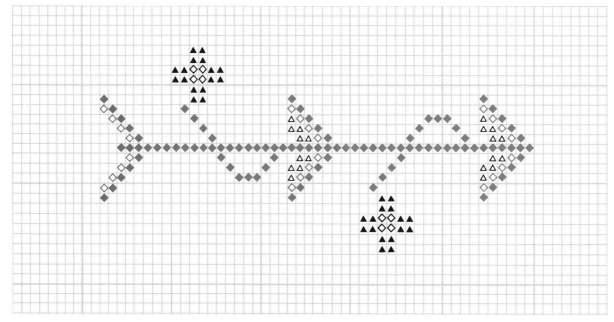

Border   light green   ◆
           dark green (blue layer)   ◇
           light brown   △
           light blue   ▲
           pink (black layer)   ◇

Deer   light brown   △
        dark brown   ○
        green   ◆

From a sampler, Mexico

Background   off-white
Design   blue   ◆
         red   △

Aztec in feeling, this would be very attractive on a man's shirt.

Color illustration page VIII.

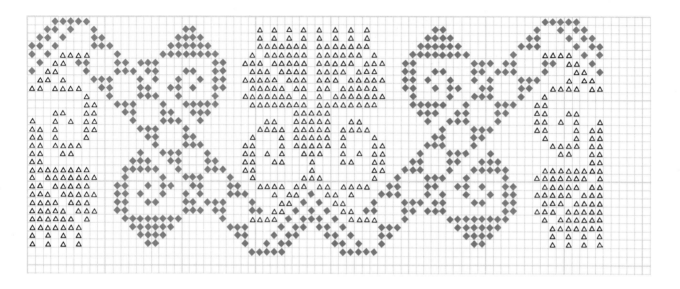

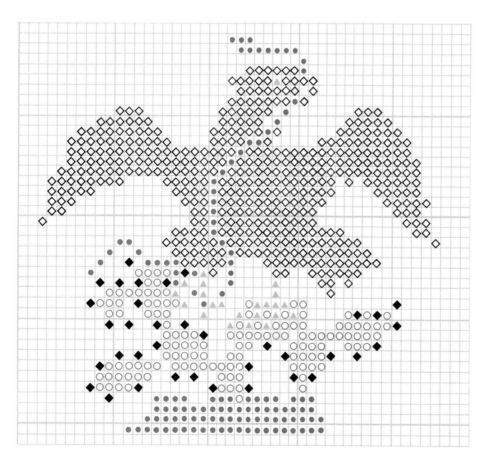

From a sampler, Mexico

Background   ecru
Design   dark brown   ◇
         yellow   ●
         green   ○
         red   ◆
         black   ▲

These eagles and serpents are found in pre-Columbian designs and later appear on early American flags.

Color illustration page VIII.

From a sampler, Guatemala

Background   ecru
Design   dark green   ○
            red   ▲

Use in either direction for a border or
an all-over design.

Color illustration page VIII.

From a sampler, Puebla, Mexico

Background   off-white
Design   light brown   ◆
         green   ▲
         orange   △
         rust   ○

This use of a "rope" to hold the design together
is characteristic of many folk art borders.
Embroidering the rope first makes the pattern
easier to follow.

Color illustration page VIII.

61

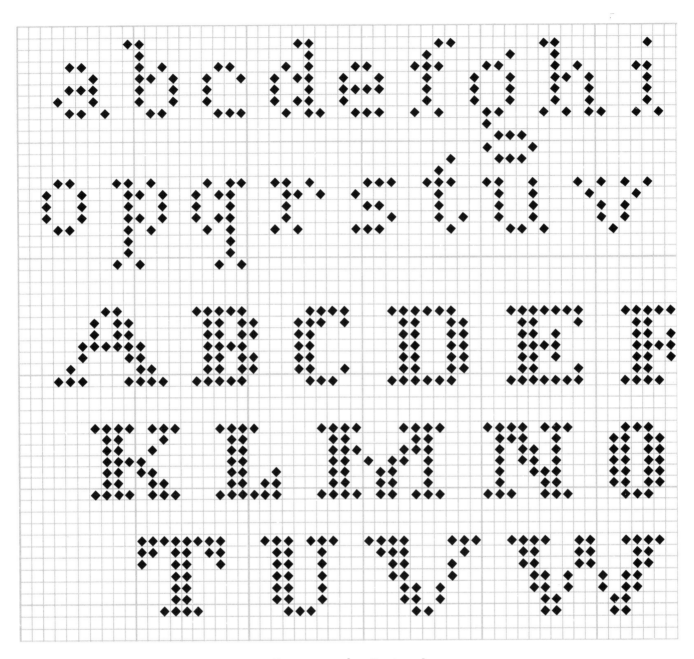

From a sampler, Guatemala

From a sampler, Puebla, Mexico

Background   even-weave linen fabric
Alphabet and numbers   black

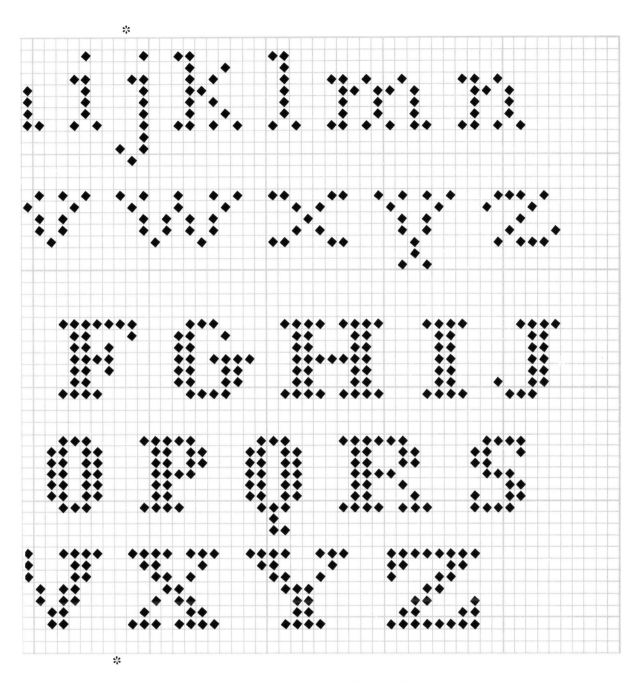

We created this lovely traditional letter and
number sampler by combining patterns from a
Guatemalan and a Mexican sampler.

Color illustration page IX.

Sections of this article appear through page 70.
See page 9 for instructions on overlapping
charts.

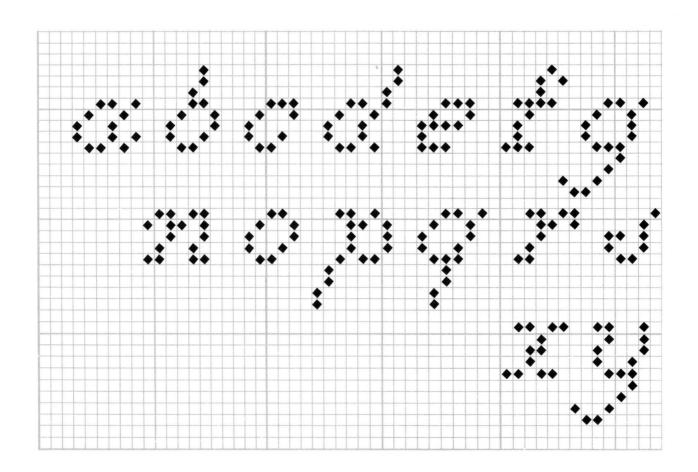

64

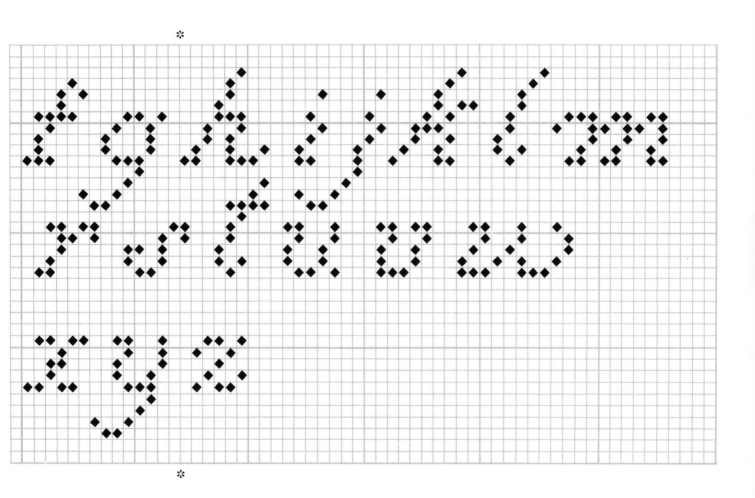

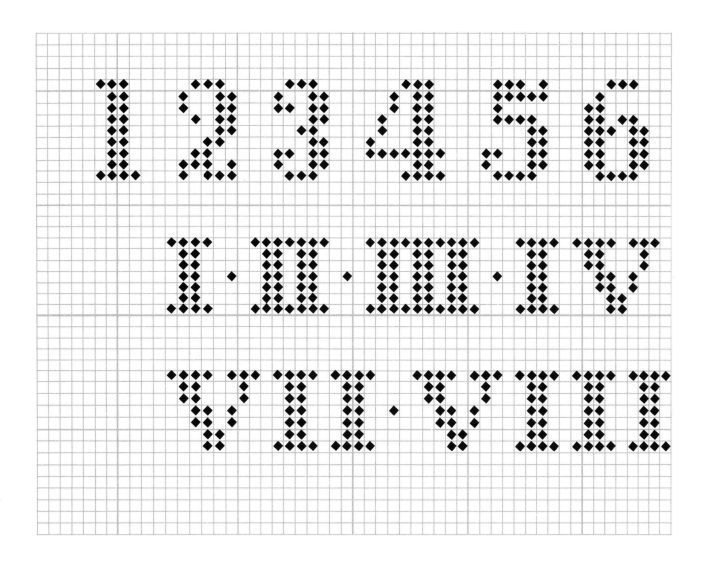

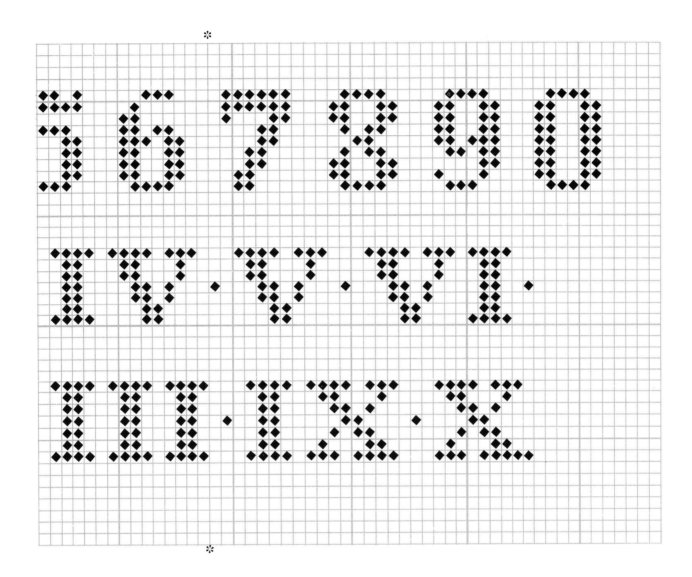

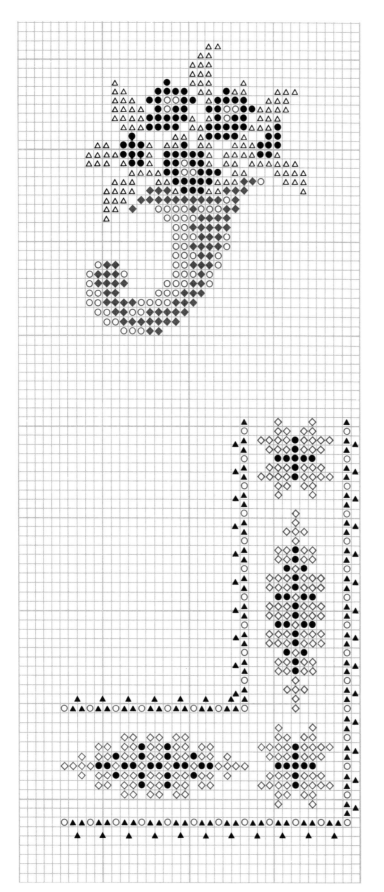

Floral design   dark green   △
                       pink   ●
                       dark yellow   ○
                       light yellow   ◆

Outside border   pink   ▲
                       dark yellow   ○
                       black   ●
                       blue   ◇

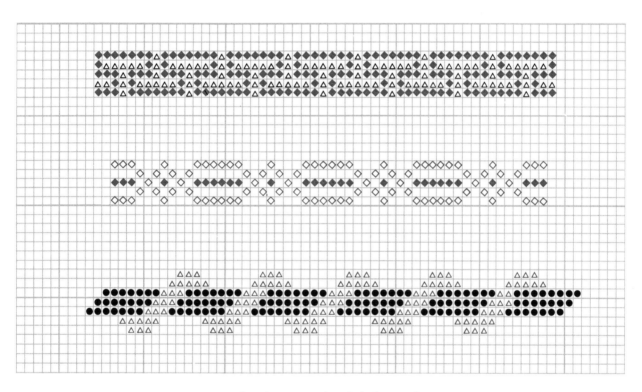

Borders between the alphabet and
number designs   pink   ◆
                  dark yellow   ○
                  light green   ●
                  dark purple   △
                  dark green   ◇
                  light yellow   △

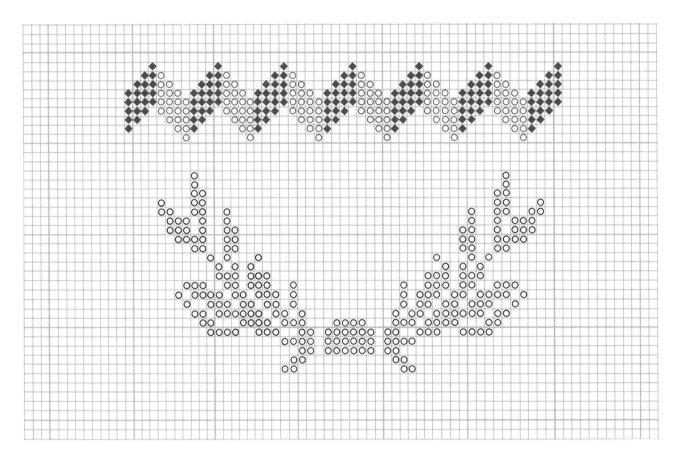

Leaves   light green   ○

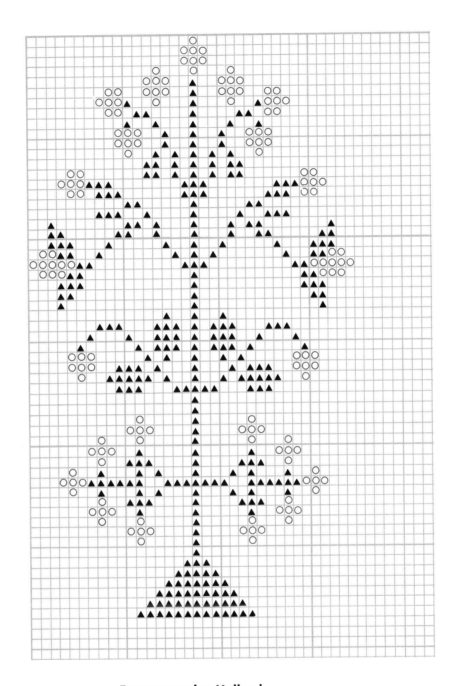

From a sampler, Holland

Background   even-weave linen fabric
Design   orange   ○
         blue   ▲

This place mat and the one following are adapted
from early nineteenth-century Dutch designs.

Color illustration page IX.

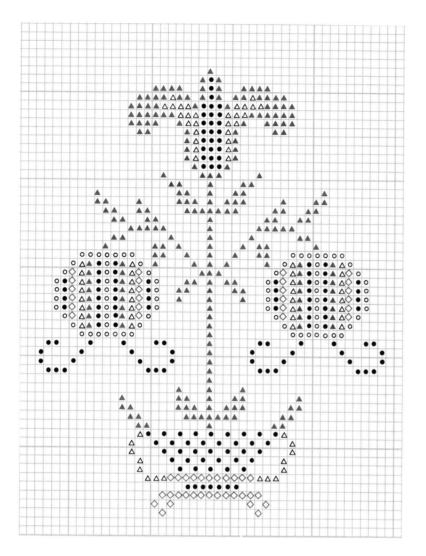

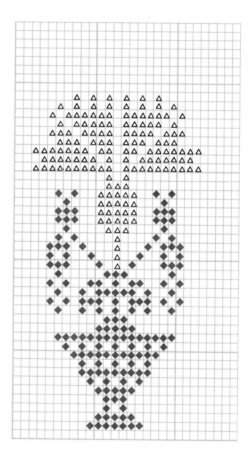

Design dark blue ▲
        light blue ◇
        pink ●
        dark red ○
        yellow △

From a bag, Mexico

Background even-weave linen fabric
Design blue ◆
        orange △

We picked up this design and the next from a Mexican bag to give you ideas for simple place mats.

Color illustration page IX.

Design   brown   ◇

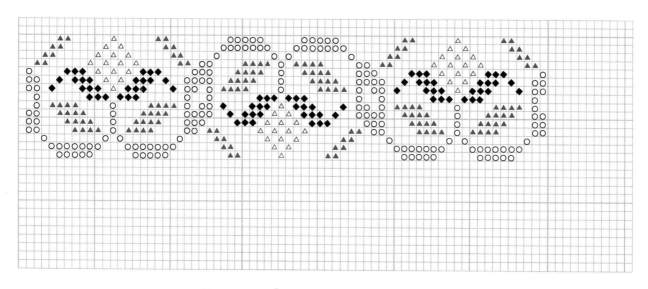

From a sampler, Guatemala

Background   white
Design   brown   ○
            red   ◆
          green   ▲
           pink   △

Another typical arrangement of rope and flowers.

Color illustration page X.

From a sampler, Puebla, Mexico

Background   white
Design   yellow   ◆
        red   ▲
        green   ○

Though this is from Mexico, its feeling
is of Central Europe.

Color illustration page X.

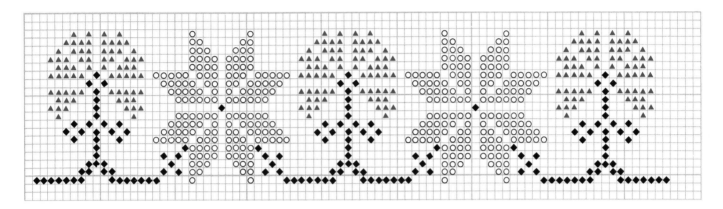

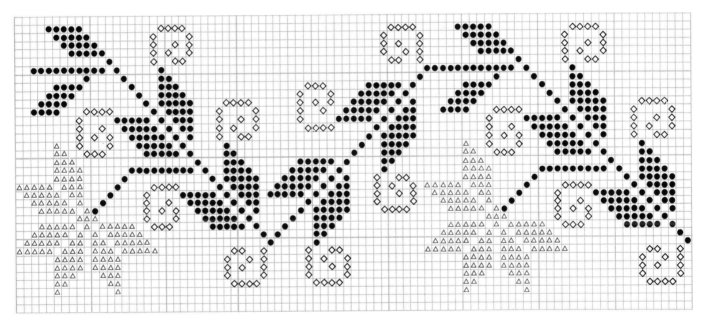

From a sampler, Puebla, Mexico

Background   white
Design   green   ●
        yellow   ◇
        maroon   △

A fresh, summery pattern.

Color illustration page X.

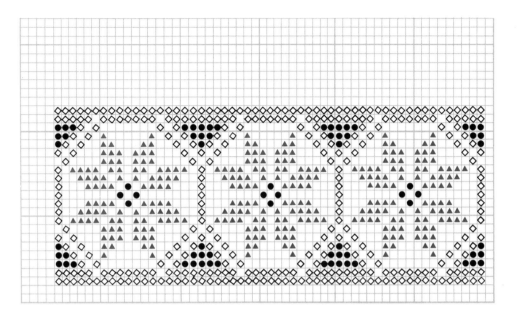

From a dress, Palestine

Background   dark green
Design   yellow   ●
     pale green   ◇
     pink   ▲

Stars in circles form a vivid row.

Color illustration page X.

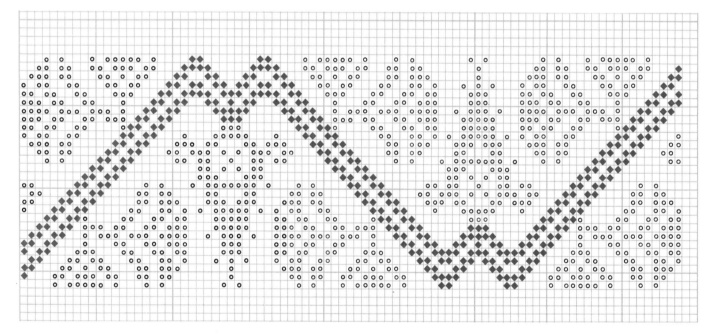

From a man's costume, Huichol tribe, Mexico

Background   white
Design   pink   ○
     red   ◆

This would be lovely on a peasant-style blouse.

Color illustration page X.

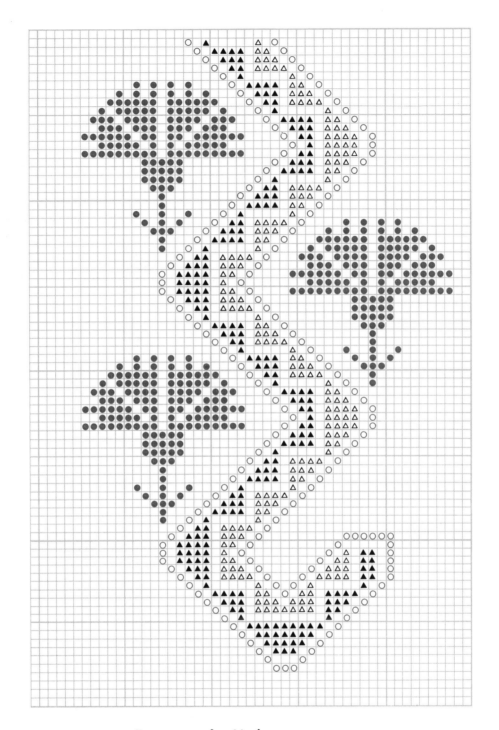

From a sampler, Mexico

Background   a closely woven linen fabric
Design   maroon   ▲
           blue   ●
           green   ○
           red   △

We worked this in cross-stitch over gauze right
onto the fabric. After the embroidery was
finished, the gauze was pulled out.

Color illustration page X.

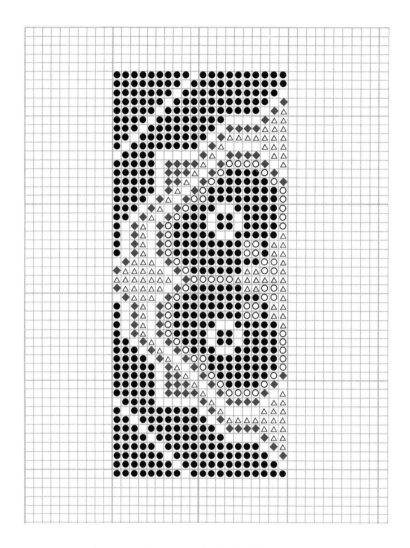

From a dress (an adaptation)

Background   monk's cloth
Design   turquoise   △
           dark green   ◆
           red   ●
           yellow   ○

Sylvia Rogers used a standard pattern to make this magnificent dress, and created her own folk-art embroidery. The dress was made out of monk's cloth material. A backstitch frames the center of the design. Apply the backstitch after the overall cross-stitch pattern is established. If you choose to work this pattern in needlepoint eliminate the backstitch.

Color illustration page XI.

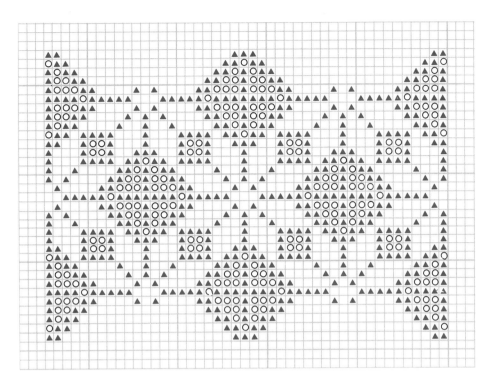

From a sampler, Guatemala

Background   ecru
Design   olive   ○
         orange   ▲

We joined the repeats of the original design to make an overall pattern, as you can do with most patterns throughout the book.

Color illustration page XII.

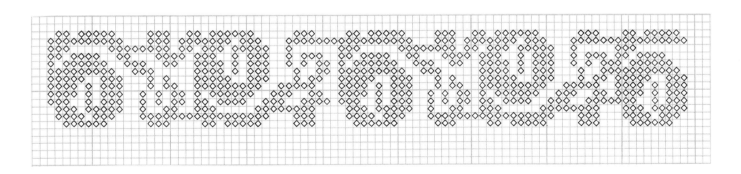

From a woman's dress, Palestine

Background   lemon-yellow
Design   maroon   ◇

This pattern requires close concentration.

Color illustration page XII.

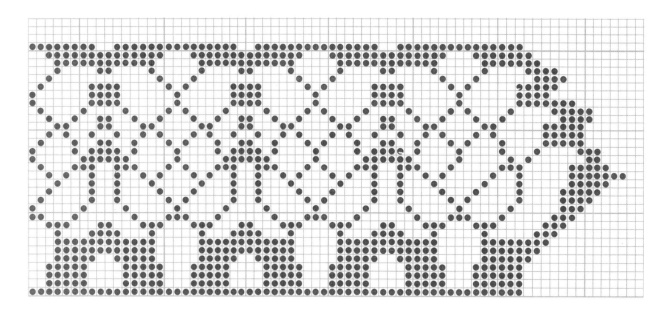

**From a woman's costume,
Moravia (Czechoslovakia)**

Background   orange
Design   gray   ●

I think of this figure as artichokes. It is fairly
complicated, and if you are a beginner you might
want to start with something easier.

Color illustration page XII.

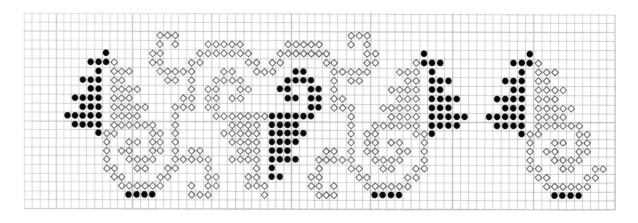

**From a man's costume, Huichol tribe,*
Mexico**

Background   green
Design   maroon   ◇
         pink   ●

This design has a symmetrical center, but
the side figures are irregular.

Color illustration page XIII.

* A tribe in Northern Mexico.

From a sampler, New Mexico

Background   mustard
Design   kelly green   ◆
         pink   ○
         maroon   ▲

Old roses from New Mexico—this type of flower occurs in folk art all over the world.

Color illustration page XIII.

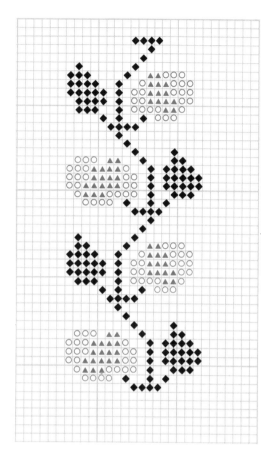

From a man's shirt, Huichol tribe, Mexico

Background   green
Design   light yellow   ▲

This tribal design has a very contemporary look.

Color illustration page XIII.

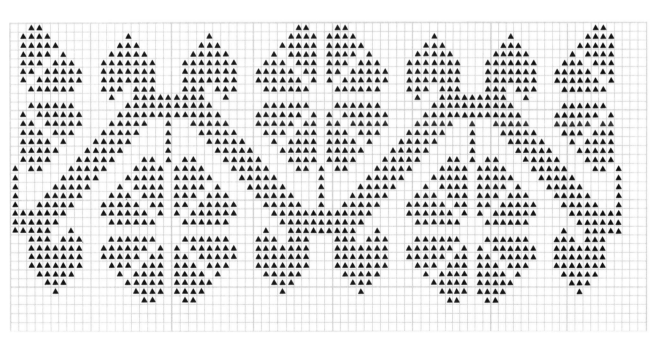

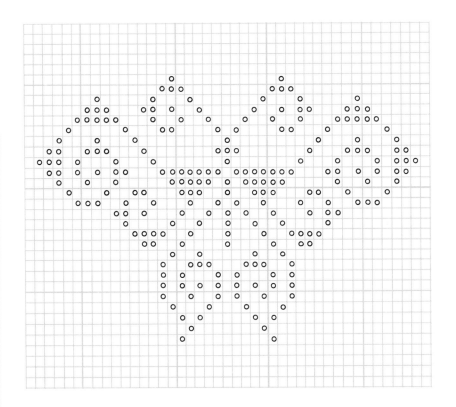

From a sampler, China

Background   green
Design   yellow   ○

To accentuate this butterfly we worked it
on rug canvas with heavy yarn.

Color illustration page XIII.

From a headshawl, Palestine

Background   bright green
Design   gold   △

Simple, typical Palestinian design.

Color illustration page XIII.

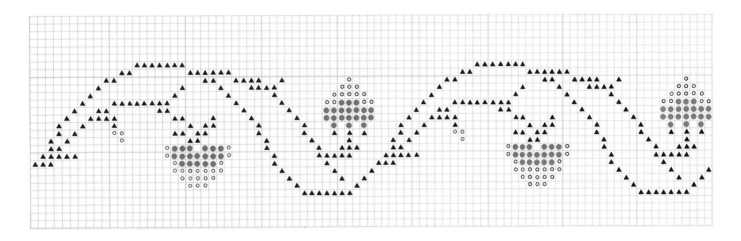

From a sampler, Mexico

Background   dark brown
Design   white   ○
         green   ▲
         red   ●

This Mexican pattern reminds me of the
strawberries of my own Swedish childhood.

Color illustration page XIII.

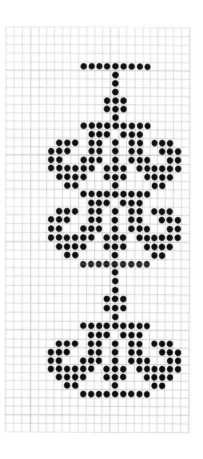

From a headshawl, Palestine
Background   blue
Design   red   ●

From an ancient culture comes this
modern-looking design.

Color illustration page XV.

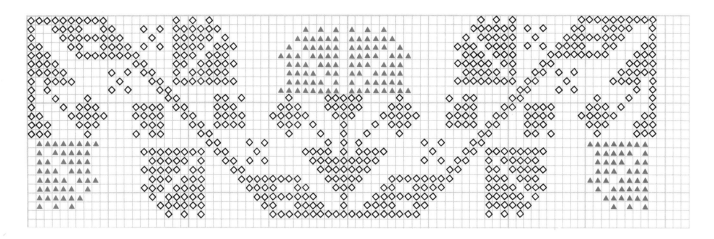

From a sampler, Guatemala

Background   blue
Flowers   red   ▲
Leaves and stems   green   ◇

These look like small Christmas trees, though the Guatemalans surely did not use them that way.

Color illustration page XV.

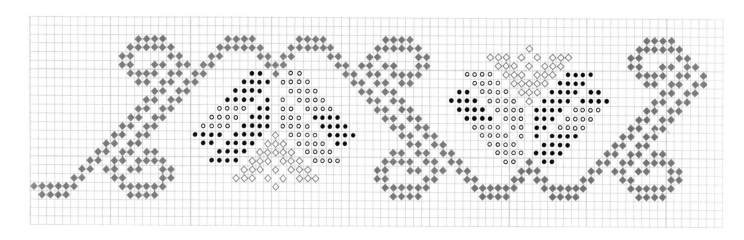

From a sampler, Mexico

Background   salmon (dark pink)
Border   dark green   ◆
Flower   light green   ○
Flower   yellow   ●
Flower   maroon   ◇

Another strong border design from Mexico.

Color illustration page XV.

From a dress, Ramallah,* Palestine

Background   red
Design   blue   ◇
        green   ●

These designs were used for ceremonial costumes, but also for everyday dress. The patterns are often named and recur over and over again in Palestinian costumes.

Color illustration page XV.

A town north of Jerusalem.

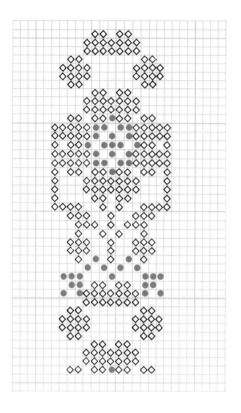

From 2 Mexican bags and a Hungarian runner

Background   even-weave linen fabric
Corner floral design: design in   yellow   △
                                brown   ●

We took the green unicorn from Hungary and the other creatures from Mexico to create this bold animal hanging. Note that the bird is shown both in cross-stitch in the hanging and, alone, in a framed needlepoint.

Color illustration pages XIV–XV.

The diagram for this design continues through page 89.

Unicorn design: green △

Color illustration page XIV.

Horse design: brown ●

Color illustration page XIV.

Deer design: blue ▲

Color illustration page XV.

From a bag, Mexico

Background   ecru canvas
Design   red   ○

This has been done in needlepoint on canvas and cross-stitch on even-weave linen fabric (see color pages XIV-XV) to show you again the adaptability of the charts.

Color illustration page XV.

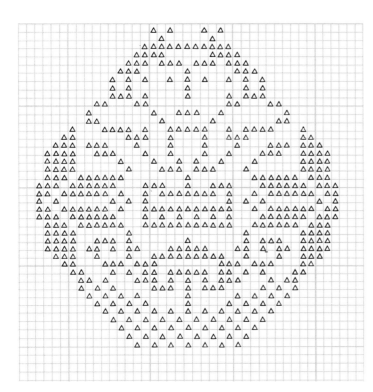

From a sampler, China

Background   ecru
Design   kelly green   △

If you like, eliminate the space between these figures and begin next repeat immediately. A flower will be formed joining the two.

Color illustration page XVI.

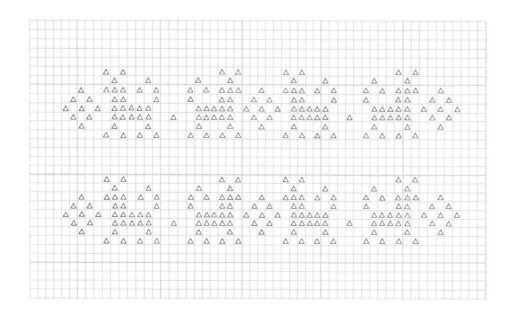

From a sampler, Mexico

Background   dark brown
Design   ecru   △

These little deer can be adapted very well on clothing, and are fun to look at.

Color illustration page XVI.

From an ankleband, China

Background   yellow
Design   brown   ●

A quite complicated but intriguing design with
a very long repeat on either side of the center.

Color illustration page XVI.

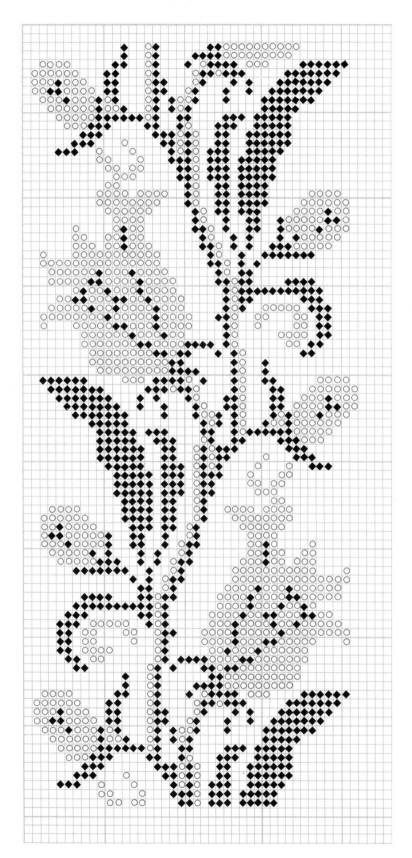

From a child's dress, Russian, Ukraine

Background   mustard
Design   pink   ○
       green   ◆

A complicated repeat pattern that takes concentration, but has a lovely old-fashioned look.

Color illustration page XVI.

From a child's dress, Romania, around 1900

Background   turquoise
Design   maroon   ◇

From the turn of the century, this is a simple stylized design.

Color illustration page XVI.

93

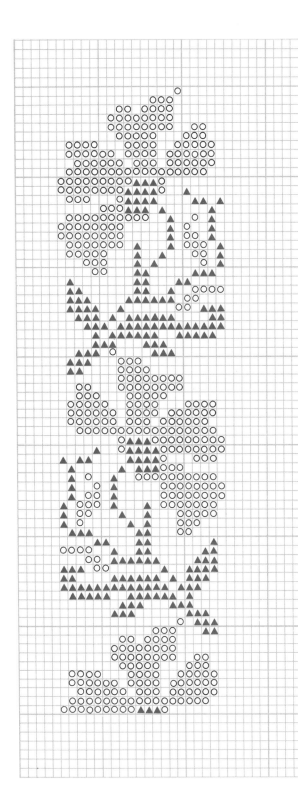

From a child's costume, Russian, Ukraine

Background yellow
Design rust ○
green ▲

The flowers in this chain reverse and can be repeated in a line or scattered at random on an overall pattern.

Color illustration page XVI.

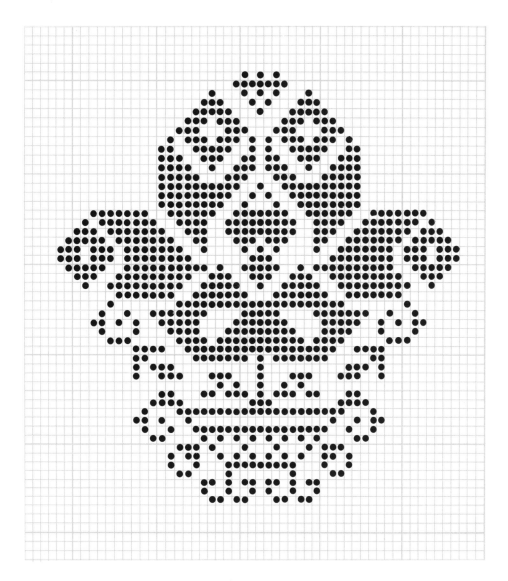

From a valance, China

Background   brown
Design   off-white (ecru)   ●

I have made a small rug in this pattern
and people argue about whether the figures
are flowers or Buddhas.

Color illustration page XVI.

About the Author

LISBETH PERRONE, one of the world's most successful authors of crafts books, was born and educated in Sweden, where she received her graduate degree in the decorative arts. She also studied in Paris and is a former director of the American Embroiderers' Guild. Her work has appeared in museums and galleries throughout the country. She now lives with her son in Santa Fe, New Mexico.